Reprint Publishing

For People Who Go For Originals.

www.reprintpublishing.com

ATONEMENT IN LITERATURE
AND LIFE

ATONEMENT IN LITERATURE AND LIFE

BY

CHARLES ALLEN DINSMORE

BOSTON AND NEW YORK
HOUGHTON MIFFLIN COMPANY
The Riverside Press Cambridge

COPYRIGHT 1906 BY CHARLES A. DINSMORE

ALL RIGHTS RESERVED

Published December 1906

To
MY FATHER
WHO THROUGH PAIN ENTERED INTO THE
GREAT RECONCILIATION

PREFACE TO NEW EDITION

Our moral battles are not between right and wrong, but between right and right; our intellectual conflicts are not between truth and error but between truth and truth, partially understood and expressed. Life would be simple and its victories easy, if the darkness was all on one side and the light on the other. The struggle is desperate and enduring because right and wrong, truth and error are on both sides.

This discussion of the Atonement is re-issued because its expositions have a vital bearing on the present conflict between the Modernists and the Fundamentalists. Although the writer is a thorough-going Modernist he believes that the Fundamentalists have one truth, which is very near the spiritual experience of men. The Modernist boasts of his social gospel, but he is teaching the most individualistic view of the Atonement which has been proclaimed in all the Christian centuries. His gospel of forgiveness deals with sin as though it were simply a sundered relationship between the individual and his God, easily mended by repentance and a return. The great mass of the people who hold the conservative position are conscious of spiritual necessities which the moral theory of the Atonement fails to meet. They look upon their transgressions as entailing certain results which repentance is powerless to remedy. They need some one to do for them what they cannot do for themselves. Therefore they cling to a doctrine of the substitutionary meaning of the cross. They believe that Jesus Christ stands in their place, takes the consequences of their sin upon himself, suffers in their stead, and thus satisfies the just demands of a violated law. To the Modernist this is artificial, it smacks of medieval law courts, it does not express God's fatherly love for his children. In this he is correct. Yet he fails to meet a need which is very deep in human nature. This need the Fundamentalist recognizes, but he interprets it in a form which is repellant to the modern mind.

In the following pages will be found, I think, the statement of a truth which the Modernist has forgotten, and which the Fundamentalist has formulated in thought-forms which are now being rapidly outgrown.

CHARLES ALLEN DINSMORE

Yale University, 1924.

PREFACE

In adding a volume to the ever increasing flood of books issued from the press of to-day, it becomes a writer to state his reasons for challenging the attention of a surfeited and much-enduring public. Especially is this true when the subject is so apparently outworn and rejected as the atonement. For this theme, once so commanding and of conceded importance, has been quite generally neglected, even by religious people, and fails to arouse more than a languid interest. The venerated interpretations now seem antiquated, and the dogma itself is in many pulpits discredited. But a doctrine which has entered so vitally into spiritual thought and experience, and which every age has explained in its own language and according to its prevailing philosophy, must contain a residuum of truth which will ever abide and reclothe itself in a fashion suited to each generation.

The word " atonement," as I shall use it, is employed to explain the method by which reconciliation with God, with life, and with one's past is achieved. My purpose is not to elaborate a dogma. This would be a thankless task. "It is not summation of doctrine that we want," says Bushnell, "we have enough of that. What we want a great deal more is something to give us greater breadth of standing and greater vitality of idea." In attempting to satisfy this need I have sought to take the gospel of reconciliation out of the stiff forms of theology and to find its essential truths as they appear in life, and life as the best minds have seen it. As this theme holds as prominent a place in literature as in religion, it has seemed to me that atonement might profitably be studied in the pages of the great seers who have been recognized by the generations as portraying most truthfully the guilt, the woe, the peace of the heart. I have no knowledge that any one has preceded me in thus approaching one of Christianity's supreme verities. This journey over an untried way has brought to view two aspects of reconciliation which are clearly revealed in literature, but which have been either sadly neglected by theology, or not given their proper place in our systems of religious thought. One becomes convinced, as he walks with those master minds who "saw life steadily and saw it whole," that the legend of Lethe with its magical waters has a deep spiritual value; and that a trust in "some soul of goodness in things evil" exercises a most important part in reconciliation. In the second section of this volume these two truths have been interpreted in their religious significance, and have been given the prominent position which belongs to them in a doctrine of reconciliation. Whatever worth there may be in these truths, and the intrinsic interest of the method pursued, constitute the writer's claim to a patient reading. I have also endeavored to indicate the distinction between the work of the historical Jesus and the Eternal Christ, although the difficulties of drawing the line of demarcation are obvious. Some confusion would have been avoided by using the phrase "indwelling God" rather than the designation "Eternal Christ." But both the Scriptures and Christian experience apply the name "Christ" to the immanent Spirit, and I have felt at liberty to follow their example in order to enforce the truth of the eternal atonement wrought by the Son of God.

To have developed the thoughts contained in this volume into a treatise, by refining definitions, by refuting critics, and by formulating a closely articulated dogma, would have been contrary to my inclinations and beyond my ability. It would also have narrowed the circle of readers to a select company of theological experts, and have made the book unattractive to that ever increasing number of readers who are interested in the deep things of the spirit, but care little for the technical language of religious science. I have therefore chosen the simpler method of sketching in broad outline truths which seem to me of superlative importance.

The following pages may be criticised for being too repetitious in statement. The fault, if it be such, arises partly from the large number of witnesses called, and partly from my desire to strongly emphasize one or two elemental truths. I have preferred to err on the side of repeated statement, rather than to fail of making the meaning perfectly clear.

I wish to acknowledge my indebtedness to Professor Edward Y. Hincks, D. D., for pertinent criticisms which have led me to express with greater accuracy and fullness the subject matter under consideration, and to the Rev. Joseph Anderson, D. D., and the Rev. Charles H. Oliphant for giving me the benefit of their trained literary tastes and their fine sense of the fitness of words and phrases in the revision of the book. These friends have put their disciplined judgments so freely at my disposal that I must take upon myself the responsibility for what is unfinished in form or erroneous in doctrine.

CHARLES ALLEN DINSMORE.

CONTENTS

PART I

CHAPTER I

Dominant Ideas in Literature and Religion

Sin, retribution, and reconciliation are the controlling ideas of both religion and literature. No religion can permanently win the assent of men which does not have a clear and sane teaching regarding the reconciliation of God and man. This reconciliation is to be studied through poets rather than through theologians. Such a method offers a new point of view, and promotes clarity of thought. As reconciliation takes place between persons, it may well be studied from life. Dante chose poets for his guides. Literature is life at its best expression. An objection answered and a limitation stated. Divine and human forgiveness analogous 3

CHAPTER II

Some Definitions and Assertions

Inattention to definition causes confusion. Reconciliation and atonement defined. Relation of the incarnation to the atonement. Phillips Brooks quoted. A fact like the atonement inseparable from theory. A doctrine of the atonement necessary 19

CHAPTER III

Homer

The theme of the Iliad is sin, retribution, reconciliation. Quarrel between Agamemnon and Achilles. Reconciled by a realization of the consequences, by repentance, by public confession, and an endeavor to make amends. Reconciliation between deity and the offender. Sin not conceived in its Christian meaning. Defilement of sin. Honor paid to the divine majesty 29

CHAPTER IV

ÆSCHYLUS

The Greek theatre at its best was the pulpit of the day. Plot of the " Oresteia." Æschylus' conception of God. The law of heredity. The retributive justice of God in history. Curse is stayed when it falls upon Orestes, a righteous man. The Furies honored. Hereditary evil checked by the moral will of a good man. The vicarious sufferer in " Prometheus Bound " . . 39

CHAPTER V

SOPHOCLES

The Shakespeare of the ancient stage. Story of " Œdipus." The inexorable divine order. What will satisfy the divine justice? Suffering endured submissively until the heart is purified and the will subdued. Œdipus is partially reconciled because evil has worked good 59

CHAPTER VI

DANTE

Latin literature omitted because conspicuously lacking in ethical and spiritual originality. The "Divina Commedia" outlined. Sin personified in Lucifer. Dante centres his theology in the love of God. Christ's death satisfies the divine justice, and remits the eternal penalties of sin for all who accept it by baptism. Man's part is performed by confession, contrition, and satisfactory deeds which expiate and purify. A Lethe for the memory. Dante is reconciled to life and its disciplines because he sees all things in God 69

CHAPTER VII

Shakespeare

Compared with Dante and Sophocles. The moral framework of the world powerfully disclosed. Macbeth. Richard III. Place of death in tragedy. Shakespeare could not permanently be satisfied with the conception of life portrayed in the tragedies. Reconciliation in "The Winter's Tale." "The Tempest" expresses Shakespeare's reconciliation with life. There is a Good Will working in all and over all. Goodness victorious over calamities. Queen Katharine. Cardinal Wolsey. Peace for the memory 89

CHAPTER VIII

Milton

Differs from Dante and Shakespeare in his treatment of sin. Emphasizes its lawlessness. Gives prominence to a neglected truth. The mind is at peace only when the results of evil are intrusted to an all-sufficient grace. Adam's agony. Michael's revelation of Christ's victory. "Paradise Regained" is based on the victory of Christ, and not on his sufferings . . . 107

CHAPTER IX

George Eliot

Only special phases of reconciliation hereafter to be considered. Reconciliation in "Adam Bede." The story. An incomplete and shadowed reconciliation. Contrition, confession, and partial satisfaction. Propitiation, but unalterable loss. Differs from Milton and Tennyson 119

CHAPTER X

Hawthorne

"The Scarlet Letter." Resemblance to Dante's "Purgatorio." Need of confession in reconciliation. Propitiation of just indignation. A greater measure of reconciliation in "The Scarlet Letter" than in "Adam Bede." 125

CONTENTS

CHAPTER XI

HOSEA AND TENNYSON

Story of Gomer's desertion. Hosea's unfailing affection. Principles of reconciliation: suffering love, repentance in view of consequences, maintenance of moral distinctions by expiatory sufferings, propitiation of holy indignation. "Idylls of the King." Arthur's holy love is checked in its passion for reconciliation by an instinctive revulsion from evil, which cannot be ignored, but must be allayed 135

CHAPTER XII

JOB, THE SUFFERING SERVANT, PSALM XVII, SYMONDS, WHITMAN, AND WHITTIER

Job's problem is to be reconciled to the providential ordering of his life. The plot of the story. The realization of God's presence and goodness is sufficient for reconciliation. An insight into results compensates the Servant for his sufferings. The beatific vision reconciles the Psalmist to life's losses. Symonds' spiritual doubts. Comte's advice. His religion of "cosmic enthusiasm." Whitman found his reconciliation with life in the faith "that a kelson of the creation is love." Whittiers' trust in an Eternal Goodness 143

PART II

CHAPTER I

DEDUCTIONS

a. Sin, retribution, forgiveness. Different characterizations of sin: its defilement, devastation, moral blindness, lawlessness. Certainty of retribution. Conscience aroused by the knowledge of the results of sin, not by the revelation of love. Conditions to be met in reconciliation: repentance, confession, satisfaction. Sanctity of moral obligations must suffer no diminution in forgiveness 155

b. Reconciliation — a larger question than forgiveness. Memory needs a Lethe. The triumph of goodness, either realized or believed in by faith, is the ground of reconciliation . . . 164

CHAPTER II

Poets and Theologians

Over against every prominent expounder of the atonement is a poet or novelist who caught the same vision and proclaimed the same essential truth. Æschylus and Anselm. Aquinas and Dante. Duns Scotus and Sophocles. Grotius and the Greek dramatists. McLeod Campbell and Hawthorne. Bushnell, Hugo, Shakespeare. Propitiation emphasized by Hosea, George Eliot, Tennyson. The ever-recurring idea that forgiveness must be righteous. Reconciliation with life the aspect of the atonement most interesting to the modern mind. Attained through a belief in Goodness in all and over all 173

CHAPTER III

What did Jesus of Nazareth do for the Forgiveness of our Sins?

Recapitulation. A well-attested fact that Jesus does save men from their sins. He arouses and deepens men's consciousness of God's moral character. He quickens and intensifies men's sense of sin by his words, actions, and consciousness. By entering into the consciousness of Jesus man realizes both the nature of sin and the holiness and love of God. Coming into the circle of the influence of Jesus, man grows into oneness with God. The cross is the focus of all the truths and forces disclosed in the life of Jesus 191

CHAPTER IV

What does the Eternal Christ do for our Reconciliation?

What forgiveness cannot do. Omission of modern writers to study the atonement in the light of man's relationship to his

xviii CONTENTS

fellows. The brother of the prodigal son. Jacob and his sons. The horror of sin is its contagion. Atonement for the memory. There can be no reconciliation with one's past without either a knowledge of how the effects of sin subserve a good purpose, or a faith that God will make human wrath to praise him. Karma. There can be no reconciliation with life without the recognition of the presence of goodness overcoming evil. Dante, Job, Milton, Whittier, Brooks. There can be no reconciliation on the part of the offended unless evil works a compensating good. God's reconciliation based on the accomplishment of his purpose. The Eternal Christ is Christianity's solution of cosmic evil. The early tendency to regard Jesus as incarnating the humanity of God. The Trinity. The perpetual sacrifice and suffering of Christ. It is a process toward victory. Promises of Christ's ultimate triumph. All things are to be put under his feet. Sin will be so dealt with that every living creature will be satisfied. This an essential part of the atonement. That God must be satisfied is the note of every great theory of the atonement. He is satisfied by the glorious accomplishment of his purposes in creation and redemption. Christ's victory is the Lethe for the memory. The indwelling Christ is literally taking our sins upon himself. His triumph is as essential a part of the atonement as his sufferings. That a Power not ourselves is working for righteousness is an observable fact. Gives a motive for action. Nature of evil. Summary 213

PART I

I

THE DOMINANT IDEAS IN LITERATURE AND RELIGION

Poet and prophet differ greatly in our loose modern notions of them. In some old languages, again, the titles are synonymous; *Vates* means both prophet and poet: and indeed at all times, prophet and poet, well understood, have much kindred of meaning. Fundamentally they are the same; in this most important respect especially, that they have penetrated, both of them, into the sacred mystery of the universe. . . . This divine mystery *is* in all times and in all places; veritably is. In most times and places it is greatly overlooked; . . . but now, I say, whoever may forget this divine mystery, the *Vates*, whether prophet or poet, has penetrated into it; is a man, sent hither to make it more impressively known to us. While others forget it, he knows it; — I might say, he has been driven to know it; without consent asked of *him*, he finds himself living in it. Once more, here is no hearsay, but a direct insight and belief; this man, too, could not help being a sincere man! Whoever may live in the show of things, it is for him a necessity of nature to live in the fact of things. — THOMAS CARLYLE.

If there were no witness in the world's deeper literature to the fact of an Atonement, the Atonement would be useless, since the formula expressing it would be unintelligible. — W. ROBERTSON NICOLL.

ATONEMENT IN LITERATURE AND LIFE

CHAPTER I

DOMINANT IDEAS IN LITERATURE AND RELIGION

THE central theme of the Bible is Sin, Retribution, and Reconciliation. It is stated immediately in the first chapters of Genesis, which describe the fall of man, announce the fearful consequences of his transgression, and promise that the seed of the woman shall bruise the serpent's head. Sin, Retribution, Reconciliation,— these three words give interest to every story in the Scriptures, interpret every psalm, form the burden of every prophecy, and explain the progressive development of God's purpose in the history of Israel and in the person of Christ.

But these great words are not the exclusive property of the Bible. They lie at the heart of all religions. Under all discrepancies of creed, every faith bears this testimony: that there is in man an uneasiness growing out of the sense of something wrong within him, and that he is to be saved from this wrongness by making proper connections with the higher powers. Along with the wrong part, man is aware of a better part within him, even though this be but a helpless germ. In seeking deliverance from the wrong "he becomes conscious that this higher part is conterminous and continuous with a MORE of the same quality, which is operative in the universe outside of him, and which he can keep in working touch with, and in a fashion get on board of and save himself when all his lower being has gone to pieces in the wreck."[1]

All religions agree that the "More" exists and acts. They differ chiefly in their interpretation of what this "More" is and how it operates. But Sin, Retribution, Reconciliation are the foundation stones upon which every faith builds its worship and its creed.

These three words are also the strands of the crimson thread running through all the world's great literature. They constitute the plot of the human drama as it has unfolded itself before the eyes of the supreme poets and novelists. They form the theme which has engrossed the thoughts of the immortals in the world of letters, from Homer to George Eliot. No other subjects are broad enough to embrace all humanity, or deep enough to defy exhaustion, or commanding enough to absorb the attention of the incomparable minds of the race.

[1] William James, *The Varieties of Religious Experience*, p. 508.

Assuming the awful fact of sin, laying tremendous emphasis on the certainty of retribution, the ever-recurrent and developing thought of the Bible is reconciliation. It is promised in the Garden of Eden; it explains the election of a unique people, its achievement is the glory of Christ, and the power of the New Testament message. The gospel is "that God was in Christ reconciling the world unto himself." Christianity does not differ from other religions in its fundamental problems, but in its more consistent and satisfying method of bringing men into harmony with God. No religion can permanently win the assent of the reason and captivate the hearts of men without having a clear, well-digested, and sane teaching of the method by which God and man are reconciled.

Theology's usual and appropriate approach to this great doctrine of the at-one-ment of humanity with Deity has been along the lines of Scripture. All the rites and ceremonies of the Hebrew faith have been searched diligently to find adumbrations of the meaning of the cross. Every text has been scanned for some hint to a solution of the great problem. Each word, sentence, metaphor, sacrifice, and institution has been placed upon the rack and tortured again and again in the hope that it would give up some unuttered secret. But biblical texts have been made to teach so many divergent views that it is no easy task to study them without prepossessions. They have formed the ground of so many fierce theological battles that little wheat is left to be gleaned from the trampled soil.

While disclaiming any thought of casting reproach upon the accepted method of studying our gospel of reconciliation, we shall approach Calvary by a new path. Poets, rather than theologians, will be our guides; dramatists will take the place of schoolmen. Again we repeat that we do not forsake the ancient way to discredit it. We shall understand prophets, apostles, theologians better when we comprehend how the deepest problems of life have been interpreted by their spiritual kindred, — the supreme seers of literature.

The advantages of this way of approach are obvious. It will offer a new point of view. Old truths become wondrously impressive when seen from an unwonted angle, fresh relationships are discerned, and unsuspected meanings are revealed. An unusual method promotes clearness of thought. Christianity cannot have escaped all distortion in its translation into the terms of Occidental speech. Metaphors which, to one bred in the temper of the East and accustomed to a rich coloring of thought, are replete with spiritual significance, are, to the more prosaic Westerner, crass and misleading. Symbols which once fitted living truths with perfect adjustment are to us but lifeless shells, archæological curiosities, whose purpose we vainly try to comprehend. The approach to the cross through the Jewish sacrificial system, with its altar forms and the " faded metaphors " of theological thought, has grave disadvantages. While it is a true and indispensable way, yet it affords many opportunities for a mind trained in other habits of thought to be led astray. Observations taken from a different point may serve to correct many errors in the ancient survey. Moreover, reconciliation takes place between persons, and may well be studied from life, — life in its richly varied aspects as seen by the most penetrating observers. We cannot understand anything when it is in isolation. Arms from a man, legs from a horse, lungs from a squirrel, skin from an elephant, a spinal column from a giraffe, made into a creature, would form an animal hideous beyond thought. Yet this has been the method of many theologians who have written upon the atonement. They have taken a verse of Oriental poetry, a metaphor from a prophetic writer, a link from one of Paul's arguments, a ceremonial from Hebrew ritual, and have attempted to fit them together into a living truth. The results have not always been edifying. Literature, on the other hand, is an interpreter of life. It is permanent only as it is true to the basal facts and sentiments of humanity. A genuinely great writer does not even control his own characters after he has created them. Having once been born, they become living beings, acting according to the inner laws of their natures. "I had more fun with Sam Weller," Dickens once said to a friend, "than any of my readers ever had. I did not know what Sam was going to say, but he would talk and I would write, and he said and did so many funny things that I was in constant merriment." This is characteristic of men of genius. They are servants to the forces of nature which work through them. A "daimon" possesses them, a god speaks through them. The evidential value of their teaching is very great, for they are sure witnesses of the elemental laws of life.

The validity of this method of inquiry is apparent. Milton affirms that a good book is the "precious life blood of a master-spirit, embalmed and treasured;" but a great book is even more: it is the distillation of an epoch, the nectar of a civilization. Homer is the essential spirit of prehistoric Greece, Dante is the "voice of ten silent centuries," Tennyson the interpreter of the struggle of faith with science. When we study the problems of sin and reconciliation in their deathless pages we are getting the testimony of an era, we are learning what has seemed true to many generations. Their affirmations therefore come clothed with august authority. They throw on old truths new light which transfigures them with impressive and unfamiliar glory.

Dante bears eloquent witness to the radiance which literature casts upon the path of life. When he would show the way by which God saves a soul lost in the dark wood of sin, he takes for his first guide Virgil, — symbol of the human reason at its best. One cannot help inquiring why he did not choose Aristotle, for whom he had an almost superstitious reverence, calling him "Master of those who know," and even declaring that "where the divine judgment of Aristotle opens its mantle, it seems to me that we should pass by the judgment of all other men." In setting aside Aristotle and selecting Virgil, Dante undoubtedly recorded his deliberate judgment that the soul finds its safest guide in the poets rather than in the philosophers. It is in poetry that reason moves in its crystalline and loftiest sphere. There it gains the surest insights. More than all others the true poet sees the dread nature of sin and its fearful reprisals. In the "Purgatorio" Dante again shows his reverence for the poets. When he and Virgil, — Reason, — baffled by the steep ascent of the Holy Mountain, needed some one to guide them, it was first the poet Sordello, and then Statius, who led the travelers' feet into right paths and their minds into hidden truth. To Dante's mind it was apparent that the supreme guides sent by Divine

Grace to reveal the fell results of sin and to show how God uses pain to purge the stains of evil, are the poets. In this his judgment accords with that of Aristophanes, who said: "Children have the schoolmasters to teach them, but when men are grown up the poets are their teachers."

Poetry, and indeed all great literature, is an interpretation of life. The permanence and rank of any production is measured by the faithfulness of its representation of life. Homer, Dante, Shakespeare live because they caught the inner spirit of an epoch or a creed and gave it a form of beauty. They were more than artists: they saw life steadily and saw it whole. They were open-eyed, and beheld the essential beneath the superficial, rightly dividing the real from the pretentious. To see deeply, and to express clearly what one sees, is the secret of all literary art. Literature manifests the inner spirit of truth. It is imperishable in proportion as life is truly revealed in it. Whatever is exaggerated, meretricious, false, is a blemish. "When I write anything which I know or suspect to be morbid, I feel as though I had told a lie," records Hawthorne in one of his note-books. The sure instincts of the race have selected here and there a poem, a drama, a story, and have lifted it out of the hurrying stream of oblivion and placed it on the serene heights among the world's treasures because it truly embodies the aspirations, the woes, the joys of life. Literature not only deals with life, but with the same aspect of life that is reflected in the Scriptures. In both we find Sin, defeating humanity, breaking the moral framework of the world; Retribution, long delayed, hidden often, yet sure as the movements of the stars; Reconciliation, obtained at great cost, but bringing peace with self, with the injured, and with God. Out of these three great realities grew what is noblest in art and profoundest in religion, and by studying them in the light of the world's ripest experiences we cannot fail of obtaining valuable spiritual insights. In looking through the eyes of the loftiest seers of the Western world upon the fundamental realities and the problems dealt with in the Scriptures, we shall see more clearly what is the distinctive contribution of Christianity to our knowledge and hope.

One accustomed to an ancient phraseology may object that such an investigation as is here proposed does not sufficiently take into account the distinction between the gropings of human reason and the certainties of a divine revelation, and may claim that our study will result only in showing the inferior conclusions of natural religion. Be it so, yet even natural religion is not a false prophet. But the distinction made is not a valid one. Unaided reason is a mere figment of thought. It does not really exist. God is in all minds. He is "the master light of all our seeing." The human reason is not hermetically sealed in a narrow inclosure. There are no fixed bounds where the natural leaves off and the supernatural begins. Choice spirits in all ages, who have been dedicated to righteousness, sensitive to truth, surrendered to the spirit, have caught sight of the gleaming framework of the world, and have been granted clear glimpses of God's way and will in human affairs. A contemplation of such insights cannot be without value.

The method of investigation we have proposed has one limitation which must be clearly recognized, if we are rightly to understand our subject. While we are perfectly correct in affirming that religion is right relationship to God and our fellows, and that personal relations with God are entered into and maintained in much the same way that they are formed and continued with other persons, and while it is indisputable that human ties afford us our surest intelligence and best analogies of divine relationships; yet there is something lying beyond all human experiences which, though incomprehensible, is supreme in its power of subduing the hearts of men. However rational we may make any doctrine of Christianity by explaining its conformity to the known laws of life, the hiding of its strength is not to be found where our explanation is most lucid, but in that twilight land where faith worships and into which the intellect cannot come with its tests and searchlights. The known is the safest and only interpreter of the unknown; but the dogmatist who imagines that all the mysteries and energies of religion lie inclosed within the little circle of his knowledge, and never lifts his eyes to the encompassing Light, whose glories, more mysterious than the darkness, must be to him forever inscrutable, has not learned where power dwelleth.

A simple illustration may best make intelligible and convincing the thought we would present. Should a chemist analyze a cupful of water dipped from the ocean, he would have definite knowledge of the constituent elements composing the sea. The same formula which would represent the contents of the cup would correctly explain the physical properties of the ocean. Yet has our chemist sufficiently comprehended the ocean when he has examined minutely the contents of his cup of water? Let him lift up his eyes and behold the sea stretching to the horizon! Let him exalt his imagination, and conceive the many waters

> "Icing the pole, or in the torrid clime
> Dark heaving;"

the ocean will then become to him

> "The image of Eternity — the throne
> Of the Invisible,"

and there will steal into his soul a sense of

vastness and majesty of which he found no suggestion in the cup. The sublimity, the feeling of immensity which gives the ocean its chief spiritual significance, makes no deposit in the small quantity of water the chemist analyzed.

In like manner we may study sin and God's forgiveness of it as interpreted by human analogies and be assured that we are pursuing a true and safe way, but how much of truth will escape our formulas! It is God who forgives! and we have an instinctive feeling that there are depths in his pardon which show no recognizable elements in human mercy. It is God who loves! and even the purest and noblest human love fails to image the glory of the divine. It is God who suffers! and the plummet of man's grief drops but a little way in the abyss of that agony. The cross of Christ must perforce be interpreted by human experience, as this affords us our only insight into its meaning, but the power of the cross lies in those depths and heights which transcend experience. All that we see gives us a sense of the unseen, and what brings the penitent to his knees, and then lifts him up and sends him on his way with exceeding joy, is not the clearness of his knowledge, but the compelling consciousness that there are abysses of sorrow which he cannot fathom, and vast ranges of grace which tower where his thought may not climb. The heart is awed in the presence of these unrevealed mysteries, is tempered and exalted by them, and finds their incomprehensible greatness an unfailing source of strength. God has many things to say to us which have not yet been uttered in human experience. His silences are even more impressive to us than his speech. We may state succinctly what the work of Christ means to us, but it would be impertinent to claim that our experience comprehends all that redemption means to God. The length and breadth and height and depth of the divine love passeth knowledge. After we have examined and tabulated all that is possible we must still exclaim: —

> "Lo, these are but the outskirts of his ways :
> And how small a whisper do we hear of him !
> But the thunder of his power who can understand ? "[1]

Yet what we do not know does not diminish the value of what we may know, nor do the heights above us make it less important that we have sure foundations for our feet. The divine must always be best understood through the human. If we have sufficient reverence, "let knowledge grow from more to more." To understand what the finest, strongest minds have found to be the chief causes of disturbance in individual and social life, and the methods by which such alienations have been remedied, of necessity must greatly help us in understanding how the sundered ties between God and man are reunited.

[1] Job xxvi, 14.

The Scriptures everywhere assume that our nature images and interprets God's; they affirm that the divine is analogous to human forgiveness. We are commanded to forgive, even as God in Christ forgave us. The two actions are conceived as having a similar quality. In a remarkable passage it is recorded that Jesus said to his disciples, "Whose soever sins ye forgive, they are forgiven unto them."[1] This power has been grasped by the Roman church as an arbitrary, ecclesiastical function; but spiritually interpreted the promise means that if a sinner has all the antecedent conditions of forgiveness so that he can be received into Christian fellowship the pardon is valid everywhere in the moral universe. True penitence merits the same reception wherever it touches the spiritual order. There is but one kind of forgiveness among moral beings, and a genuine human pardon is an interpretation of God's own action. What is thus remitted on earth is remitted in heaven, and what cannot be forgiven on earth is everywhere retained.

[1] John xx, 23.

II

SOME DEFINITIONS AND ASSERTIONS

Show me a tenet which mankind have in every age been labouring to demonstrate; in behalf of which genius has piled up structure after structure of massy argument; in reference to which each period has been conscious of the failure of the preceding, and yet set itself to try another turn of skill; let me see that this untiring industry has applied itself to the proof by opposite and distinctive methods, and after exploring in vain every road of thought is fresh and unexhausted still; and I at once recognise in that doctrine the very happiest order of truth, and precisely because, all men trying, no man can prove it. No amount, no duration of failure sufficing to throw it off, what shall I infer but that it is one of those things, not which the mind must believe because it is proved, but which it must prove because it must believe. — JAMES MARTINEAU.

CHAPTER II

SOME DEFINITIONS AND ASSERTIONS

As inattention to definitions is ever a prolific source of mental confusion and obscure writing, it will aid our investigation to tarry for a moment to make clear the sense in which some important words will be used.

Reconciliation is the perfect repose of the mind in a restored and harmonious relationship. The persons reconciled are able to look upon the past, the present, and the future with joyful acquiescence. We shall use the word to denote not only a knitting together of sundered ties, but also all those feelings of trust, complacency, gladness which are attendant upon complete union of spiritual beings. The word has both an objective and a subjective meaning. It includes the outer relationship and the inner peace resulting from the renewal of friendship. It is thus a more comprehensive word than forgiveness, for we may forgive when we cannot contemplate past and present conditions with satisfaction. In the following pages forgiveness will be employed to express the free pardon of transgression. The forgiven one comes again into right relationships with the one injured, good will is unrestrained, and confidence is restored. When the thought is not only the renewed relationship but the perfection of those feelings which result from two persons being in perfect accord, then the word employed will be reconciliation. Reconciliation includes forgiveness, but has a still larger significance.

Atonement signifies the method by which reconciliation is established. In theology it is often used to describe merely the way forgiveness is attained; here it is employed as the term for expressing all that has been done by God through Christ to establish perfect harmony between man and his Creator. It is the elect word to cover man's philosophy of Christ's work of redemption.

Atonement will be discussed, not as a three-hour transaction on Calvary, nor as a work performed during thirty-three radiant years. It began with time, and closes with the end of days. In this all-embracing sense the word will be employed.

The atonement may seem to some an outworn theme. The emphasis of the pulpit to-day is certainly not put upon redemption and reconciliation. "It seems to me," writes Phillips Brooks, "as if the Christian world to-day was entering upon a movement, nay, had already entered upon and gone far in a movement which is certainly to be no less profound and full of meaning than the great Protestant Reformation of three centuries ago. The final meaning really is the nearness of the soul of God to the soul of man, and of the soul of man to God. It is the meaning of the Incarnation."[1] Undoubtedly a result of our modern religious thinking has been to emphasize the constant and consecrating union of God with humanity, which discloses relationships which ever have been and ever shall be, and thus interprets the life of Christ as a symbol of a perpetual divine life with men, instead of an isolated event out of the range of human possibilities. This new movement teaches that the special incarnation in Christ was in the interest of a universal incarnation in humanity. It approaches the age-long problem of reconciliation with the mighty assertion of essential unity of the Divine and human natures and the ever-present good will of God, and it peremptorily discards all mechanical and artificial methods of restoring right relations. This larger and deeper vision is an inestimable gain. The chief danger in this inspiring new movement has already made itself manifest. Many religious leaders go no further than the affirmation that we are one with God by nature. To them the inherent dignity of man is the whole gospel, whereas the promise and power of the New Testament message is that we

[1] Allen's *Life of Phillips Brooks*, vol. ii, p. 502.

may attain yet more, even an ethical and spiritual unity with God through his grace freely offered. The burden of the gospel is that the Infinite Father is sparing no cost to bring us into this perfect oneness with himself. Reconciliation, ethical and spiritual union with God, must be the elemental significance of the new theology as of the old, if the newer thought is to have vitality. The Incarnation is not to be set over against the Atonement. It is as Atonement that the Incarnation reveals its fullest significance. Interest has not shifted from Calvary to Bethlehem; Christianity's symbol is not to become the manger instead of the cross. The religious thinker must still take his stand at the cross, for it is there only that all the lines of redemption converge and Christian verities are seen in the right perspective. Not what man is by nature, but what he can become through grace, is Christianity's enduring message.

But why add another to the many explanations of the work of Christ in reconciliation? Every great theory, propounded by wise men and defended by learned schools, has been overthrown. At best it was only a half truth, belittling rather than exalting the cross, making a supreme vital fact into a jejune and musty dogma at once hard to understand and barren of spiritual results. Every student will sympathize with Jowett's exclamation that " the cross of Christ is to be taken up and borne: not to be turned into words, or made a theme of philosophical speculations." Exaggerated emphasis upon words and definitions has been fruitful of nothing but theological controversy. Those battlefields are the "arid Soudan of Christian teaching." Yet the blighting fault of ancient controversialists was not their efforts to interpret religious experiences, but a stubborn determination to force their formulas into another man's mind and soul. In truth we cannot put any two facts together without having a theory of their relationship. Much less can we bring the deep need of our souls face to face with the cross of Christ without having our minds powerfully stimulated to explain the wonderful significance of the regenerating experience. The intellect can no more refrain from seeking to comprehend the nature and meaning of the forces entering into the religious life, than a healthy stomach can receive food without attempting to assimilate it. If it is a choice between a good digestion and a bad one, we prefer the good. Similarly the mind must feed itself on the truths wrought out in life, and as the imperative necessity is laid upon it to interpret its experiences, it prefers the best possible explanation. Truth is inseparable from life. It springs from it as light and power from the sun. Christian doctrines are the laws of the religious life, and are no more to be sneered down than are the scientific attempts to explain the methods of nature. It is only when what God hath joined together man puts asunder, and truth is separated from life, that it becomes dead. It is the building of unsightly, mechanical superstructures upon isolated texts — and thus away from the soil where common life is spent — that has brought elaborate statements of Christian truth into disrepute.

But truth is not merely the product of life; it reacts upon life and nourishes it as the leaves of a tree enrich the ground which produces them. The individual can get along very well with a genuine experience crudely interpreted, but the church has a gospel to proclaim. She has an appeal to make to the intelligence. She reaches men's hearts and wills through their minds, and she must choose between a language moulded by the best thought of the times and saturated with its noblest spirit, and a speech that is repellent through its barbaric crudity. No permanent, vigorous, intelligent church or Christian civilization can be built up unless the facts and forces of the religious life can be interpreted in the accredited thought of the day. As a brilliant writer has stated, "A fact like the atonement can be separated from theory of some kind only by a suffusion of sentiment in the brain, some ethical anæmia, or a scepticism of the spiritual intelligence." Thought surrounds every deed as the atmosphere envelops the earth. Doctrines are the grappling irons which the mind throws to the crag above to help it in its steep ascent. Men are permanently organized and held together by truth, not by emotion.

III
HOMER

Much have I travell'd in the realms of gold,
    And many goodly states and kingdoms seen;
    Round many western islands have I been
Which bards in fealty to Apollo hold.
Oft of one wide expanse had I been told
    That deep-brow'd Homer ruled as his demesne;
    Yet did I never breathe its pure serene
Till I heard Chapman speak out loud and bold:
Then felt I like some watcher of the skies
    When a new planet swims into his ken;
Or like stout Cortez when with eagle eyes
    He stared at the Pacific — and all his men
Look'd at each other with a wild surmise —
    Silent, upon a peak in Darien."
        KEATS: *On First Looking into Chapman's Homer.*

CHAPTER III

HOMER

In our study of literature with reference to the principles upon which reconciliation is effected, we come first of all to the Iliad. It is not necessary for us to enter into the vexed question of authorship. The debate whether the swiftly moving story of wrath and valor was the song of blind Homer or a harmony of many singers, has no bearing upon our investigation. From one or many, it is a vivid picture of the conceptions, passions, customs of a primitive people. It is the clear voice of an epoch. Fortunately also it was not written with the ulterior purpose of exploiting any theory either of politics or religion. Virgil is the poet of the Roman Empire, constraining the flow of his song to glorify Italy and the great Augustus. Dante puts into a form of vivid and deathless beauty the august theology of the Middle Ages. Milton avowedly seeks to justify the ways of God to man. Homer, on the contrary, is unhampered by any of the necessities of an advocate. He simply is telling a story, and this permits him to give free rein to his artistic and ethical impulses. His sole restraint is that he must paint so true a picture of men and gods that he shall not violate the best instincts of his hearers. When he treats of that ever-present theme in literature, reconciliation, he has no conscious purpose of framing a theology or of pointing a moral. It is because in his glowing pictures of life he assumes certain fundamental principles as essential to honorable living that his testimony has so great worth. The Iliad makes no pretence of being a history of the Trojan War. It is merely a chapter torn from the record of that prolonged struggle. When the last book is finished devoted Troy is still standing; effeminate Paris holds in full possession Helen's fatal beauty; the petulant Achilles, whose death has been plainly predicted, rests in his tent. Nothing is complete but the tale of Achilles' deadly wrath, its woeful consequences, and his final reconciliation with Agamemnon.

Sin, Retribution, Reconciliation, — this is the theme of the Iliad. Not sin in our modern sense, indeed; but still a foolish infraction of right personal relations entailing fateful consequences. The very first lines strike the keynote and unfold the plot.

> "O Goddess! sing the wrath of Peleus' son,
> Achilles; sing the deadly wrath that brought
> Woes numberless upon the Greeks, and swept
> To Hades many a valiant soul, and gave
> Their limbs a prey to dogs and birds of air, —
> For so had Jove appointed, — from the time

> When the two chiefs, Atrides, king of men,
> And great Achilles, parted first as foes." [1]

The main features of the story which runs through the twenty-four books are these: Chryses, priest of Apollo, comes to Agamemnon, king of the Greeks, who is beleaguering Troy, and asks the return of his captive daughter, offering at the same time an appropriate ransom. The warrior gruffly refuses, whereupon the priest prays to the god Apollo, who in anger showers down for nine days his pestilence-bearing arrows on the Greeks. The seer Calchas declares that the wrath of the god will not be appeased until Agamemnon restores to the aged priest his daughter. At this announcement —

> "Wide ruling Agamemnon greatly chafed.
> His gloomy heart was full of wrath, his eyes
> Sparkled like fire." [2]

Yet to save his people from destruction he gives up the "fair-cheeked maid," Chryseis, and in what he afterwards describes as a fury sent by Fate, takes from Achilles for a recompense the maiden Briseis, whom that impetuous warrior dearly loved and who had been awarded to him as a prize of war. In sullen anger Achilles retired to his tent and refused to have further part in the war. From that hour the siege went against the Greeks and they were driven to their ships, expect-

---

[1] Bryant's translation.
[2] *Ibid.*, book i, 134.

ing that on the morrow crested Hector with the Trojan host would vanquish them and burn their fleet. The stress of battle exhausted Agamemnon's anger and cleared his vision, so that he perceived his fateful folly in alienating Achilles. In a council of war the king acknowledges his fault and offers to appease the wrath of the offended chief —

> "With gifts of priceless worth. Before you all
> I number them, — seven tripods which the fire
> Hath never touched, six talents of pure gold,
> And twenty shining caldrons, and twelve studs
> Of hardy frame, victorious in the race.
>
> . . . .
>
> Seven faultless women skilled in household arts,
> Damsels in beauty who excel their sex.
> These I bestow and with them I will send
> Her whom I took away, — Briseis, pure."[1]

Moreover Achilles was to have the first chance in the division of the spoil of Troy; he might choose twice ten young Trojan women, beautiful beyond their sex, save Helen; he might become Agamemnon's son-in-law, having the choice of the king's three daughters, and instead of endowing the bride, Agamemnon would give as a dowry seven cities with thronged streets.

Three of Achilles' dearest friends, Ulysses, Ajax, and Phœnix, bear to him this offer of reconciliation; but the doughty warrior, still nourishing his hurt, refuses to be appeased: —

[1] Bryant's trans., ix, 144 ff.

> "I leave him to himself
> To perish. All-providing Jupiter
> Hath made him mad. I hate his gifts; I hold
> In utter scorn the giver." [1]

The battle is again renewed, and the Greeks are driven once more to their ships by the Trojans, who attempt to set fire to the fleet. Patroclus, Achilles' bosom friend, can endure inactivity no longer, and tearfully asks leave to don Achilles' armor and lead his myrmidons to the relief of the Greeks. Permission is given, and he performs prodigies of valor, carrying the battle to the very walls of Ilium, where he is slain.

Achilles is inconsolable at this loss, and the desire for revenge and the knowledge of the sore straits of his former comrades-in-arms burn up his sullen resentment.

> "Along the beach the great Achilles went,
> Calling with mighty shouts the Grecian chiefs.[2]"

They assembled in council, and Achilles renounced his enmity. When Agamemnon pressed the offer of gifts upon him, he treated it as a matter of small importance. But this the judgment of the king would not allow. The maid Briseis was restored and with her were given the presents Agamemnon had promised. Donning the armor forged by Vulcan, Achilles led the attack, defeated Hector, and dragged the body at his chariot wheels. With the pathetic picture of

---

[1] Bryant's trans., ix, 468 ff.   [2] Ibid., xix, 47.

the aged Priam begging the mangled form of his son and bearing it away by night from the tent of the victor, the poem ends.

The factors upon which this reconciliation depended are very evident. Both chieftains were hot-tempered and in the wrong. There could be no reuniting of their severed friendship until each was brought to a better frame of mind. This was accomplished in both by seeing the disastrous consequences of their folly. Agamemnon saw his army defeated through lack of Achilles' aid, and Achilles beheld the destruction of his former friends and the death of Patroclus, dear to him as his own life. The fearful results entailed by this stubborn foolishness brought both to repentance. Both offered public confession in the council of the chiefs. Agamemnon made every amend in his power, and Achilles did the same by entering the battle, although the gods had foretold that it meant for him certain death.

There was on the part of each repentance because of the direful results of their wrong, a public confession, and an earnest endeavor to make full amends. Yet their reconciliation was shadowed by the thought that full atonement could not be made. Achilles' deadly wrath had indeed brought —

> "Woes numberless upon the Greeks, and swept
> To Hades many a valiant soul."

For this loss no restitution could be made.

Reconciliation between an offended Deity and sinful man proceeds on the same principles. The Supreme in Homer is a nature deity whose character is expressed in all the forces of the physical and moral world, both good and evil. He is the source of all things. He has many manifestations, revealing himself in the nine great Olympians, in the smaller gods, in Fate, in laws which make for righteousness, and in whimsical, arbitrary decrees.

With such a conception of the Supreme, sin certainly cannot have its full Christian meaning. It is rather a blind folly which leads man to his undoing. Often it comes from God himself, for Agamemnon declares that the cause of his offense against Achilles was from above: —

> "Yet was not I the cause,
> But Jupiter, and Fate, and she who walks
> In darkness, dread Erinnys. It was they
> Who filled my mind with fury in the hour
> When from Achilles I bore off his prize.
> What could I do? A deity prevails
> In all things, Atè, mighty to destroy,
> Daughter of Jove, and held in awe by all."[1]

But when one foolishly does wrong, either from willfulness or because entangled in Atè's net, how shall he atone to the heavenly powers? The first book of the Iliad gives an interesting answer. Agamemnon had angered Apollo by refusing to hear the prayer of his priest for the restoration of

[1] Bryant's trans., xix, 103 ff.

the captive maiden Chryseis. The consequence of the wrong in the eyes of the king is twofold, — defilement and guilt. To be rid of the first the warrior purified the camp and cast the pollution in the sea. It was the same instinct as that which caused the Hebrew to send the scapegoat into the wilderness, and which the Christian expresses by the water of baptism. To remove the guilt they made every possible amends. Ulysses restored the fair-cheeked maiden to her father, sacrifices were offered, and the youths chanted forth high anthems to the Archer of the skies, who, as he listened to the strains, softened his stern mood.

In this simple incident we have a very clear setting forth of the primitive impulses which arise when one would atone for sin. When the offense is between man and man, there is repentance in view of the consequences of the fault, acknowledgment, and such restitution as is possible. When the evil is against God there is a sense on the part of the offender of the defilement of his sin. He casts its filth away, and then performs a deed intended to exalt the majesty of the divine government which he has dishonored.

IV
ÆSCHYLUS

The old Injustice joys to breed
Her young, instinct with villanous deed;
The young her destined hour will find
To rush in mischief on mankind:
She too in Atè's murky cell
Brings forth the hideous child of hell,
A burden to the offended sky,
The power of bold impiety.

But Justice bids her ray divine
E'en on the low-roofed cottage shine;
And beams her glories on the life
That knows not fraud, nor ruffian strife.
The gorgeous glare of gold, obtained
By foul polluted hands, disdained
She leaves, and with averted eyes
To humbler, holier mansions flies;
And looking through the times to come,
Assigns each deed its righteous doom.
ÆSCHYLUS.

CHAPTER IV

ÆSCHYLUS

WE turn from Homer — with his rudimentary moral impulses — to Æschylus and Sophocles, through whose eyes the Greeks first saw clearly the inexorableness and grandeur of that moral order which penetrates and constrains human action. During the intervening centuries the nation has grown in wisdom, and we shall find profounder views and more reasoned judgments. The rise of the Greek drama, like the development of the stage in Shakespeare's time, was the result of a thorough awakening of the national mind in the presence of impending calamity. The threatened invasion of the Persian hordes, checked at Marathon and Salamis, so deeply stirred the Greeks that their sobered and exultant life could not but register itself in phenomenal thoughts and deeds. Great literature follows closely in the wake of great events. The stimulated patriotism and the steadied and enriched moral consciousness of the people found their highest interpretation and their surest guidance upon the stage. The Greek theatre at its best was the pulpit of the day. It not only expressed the profoundest emotions of the nation, it turned them into right channels of thought and action. What the prophets were to the Hebrew, the dramatists were to the Greek. They revealed the moral significance of the supreme events of the national history, and set forth in vivid and impressive scenes the fundamental truths of religion.

The most conspicuous names associated with the Greek stage are those of Æschylus, Sophocles, and Euripides. Æschylus was the founder of the drama; Sophocles carried it to its culmination; with Euripides it began to decline. As the latter, with all his unquestioned power, sees nothing of religious significance that does not find more powerful expression in the first two, we shall confine our attention to them. Both are mighty preachers of righteousness.

Of the seventy-eight plays which Æschylus wrote only seven have come down to us. We cannot but feel this to be an irreparable loss. His mind dwelt habitually in the loftiest realm of moral truth, and what was native to him he expressed in words and scenes of such simplicity and grandeur that those forgotten plays refute Emerson's confident generalization: —

> "One accent of the Holy Ghost
> A heedless world has never lost."

Æschylus connected his weightier plays in a series, because only thus could he worthily disclose the final working out of his principles. Fortunately, of the seven plays which we possess, three, Agamemnon, Chæphoræ, and the Eumenides form a trilogy, commonly called the " Oresteia." This great trilogy is the dramatist's masterpiece, and as it was not written until two years before his death, contains his matured convictions. Before considering its architectonic thought we may profitably recall the outlines of the mythical tale upon which the drama is based.

The wife of Atreus, king of Argos, was wronged by Thyestes, his brother. Atreus, pretending to forgive him, invited him to a banquet at which was served to the guests the flesh of Thyestes' own children. The horror-stricken father invoked a curse upon the house of Atreus, praying that all might perish even as had his own children. The two sons of Atreus, Agamemnon and Menelaus, married the daughters of Leda, Clytemnestra and Helen. Paris, enamored of Helen's beauty, violated the laws of hospitality and carried her off to Troy. To avenge the deed, Agamemnon led the hosts of the Greeks against the city of Priam. Agamemnon, though a great king, was not without his frailties, and one day in hunting shot a stag sacred to Artemis, boasting that he was a better hunter than she. The angered goddess caused foul weather to delay the fleet at Aulis many days, and the prophet Calchas announced that the ships could not sail unless the king offered up his daughter Iphigenia in sacrifice. This Agamemnon reluctantly did; the fleet sailed; and after ten years he returned to his home victorious over the Trojans. On his arrival he found that his wife Clytemnestra had been unfaithful to him with Ægisthus, son of Thyestes. Clytemnestra sternly chided him for their daughter's death, and in revenge slew him in his bath. Orestes, their son, at the bidding of Apollo, killed his mother, but was immediately pursued by the avenging Furies, until his case was tried before a jury of Athenians, and Pallas Athene pronounced him cleared of his guilt. The enraged Furies were propitiated by the promise of high honors to be given by the Athenians, and so were no longer Erinnyes, Furies; but Eumenides, gracious goddesses. Thus the curse upon the house of Atreus was stayed.

To us this may seem an idle tale. To Æschylus these traditions of his country embodied truths of utmost importance to its perpetuity; they were the means, ready at hand, of impressing the sternest and most august moral teachings; they offered a superb vehicle for the communication of his message, for were not these very traditions created and moulded by the thought and experience of centuries? Did they not express life in its essential features as the common people believed it? How far the poet credited the historical validity of the narrative he employed is unimportant to inquire. The immemorial laws of God which they visualized he believed with the full intensity of his nature.

We shall best understand Æschylus' conception of sin, retribution, and reconciliation in the light of his idea of the nature of God. We have no reason to suppose that the poet questioned the existence of the gods of his country, whether supernal or infernal, but his mind was too great and sane to rest in such a conglomerate multiplicity. He found a higher unity in a Supreme Righteousness to which both gods and men were subject. Of this Eternal Reality Zeus is the loftiest manifestation and therefore worthy of all honor. In "Prometheus Bound," Zeus is sketched as an insolent usurper, but in "Agamemnon" the poet's thought is loftier.

> " Zeus — if to the Unknown
>   That name of many names seem good —
> Zeus, upon Thee I call.
>   Through the mind's every road
> I passed, but vain are all,
> Save that which names thee, Zeus, the Highest One." [1]

According to the mythology of the day, which Æschylus used, Zeus was the third ruler of the gods and men. Uranus had been overthrown by Cronus, and he in turn by Zeus. The thought hidden under the mythological veil is that the first stage of the world's history was the reign of physical forces, followed by a period of har-

[1] Morshead's trans.

mony and joy — the golden age, — but the present is a day of good and evil over which is an inexorable divine government. This Power Supreme may as well be called Zeus as by any other name. But whatever the representative word chosen, the highest is Righteous. Naught can escape his open-eyed justice.

> " For never with unheedful eyes,
>   When slaughtered thousands bleed,
> Did the just powers of Heaven regard
>   The carnage of th' ensanguined plain.
> The ruthless and oppressive power
> May triumph for its little hour;
>   Full soon with all their vengeful train
>   The sullen Furies ride,
> Break his fell force, and whirl him down
> Through life's dark paths, unpitied and unknown." [1]

The same unerring sight that observes the multitude detects the individual in the violation of the right: —

> " To Troy the shining mischief came;
>   Before her, young-eyed pleasures play ;
> But in the rear with steadfast aim
>   Grim-visaged Vengeance marks his prey." [2]

These afflictions which inevitably follow wrong-doing are not merely the recoil of the disturbed equilibrium of the moral world; they chasten and instruct man. The Supreme is benignant as well as righteous.

> " 'T is Zeus alone who shows the perfect way
>   Of knowledge. He hath ruled
> Men shall learn wisdom, by affliction schooled.

Potter's trans.   [2] Ibid.

> In visions of the night, like dropping rain,
> Descend the many memories of pain
> Before the spirit's sight ; through tears and dole
> Comes wisdom o'er the unwitting soul —
> A boon, I wot, of all Divinity,
> That holds its sacred throne in strength, above the sky ! "[1]

Nowhere in the early literature of the world, if we except perhaps a passage in Ezekiel (chap. xviii), is there a more majestic assertion of the justice of God than in the third chorus of the Agamemnon.

To Æschylus divine justice was not a vague spiritual intuition, a magnificent poetical generalization. It was attested by two infallible witnesses,— the law of heredity and the providential retribution disclosed in history.

The mystery of heredity has been of absorbing interest to men from far antiquity. No sooner does a man begin to exercise his conscious freedom than he finds himself restrained like Hamlet by limitations of temperament, or like Cassius hurried into indiscretions by a "rash humour" for which he feels he is not responsible. Whence came these intractable elements, these fatal weaknesses ? What malignant fiend threw the dark drop into the red current of our blood? By what process can it be worked out? The wisdom of to-day explains the mystery by what is called a law of heredity. Yet our wisest teachers feel that here they are using words without

[1] Morshead's trans.

much knowledge. The fact of heredity we know, but the methods of its operation are as veiled to us as to our fathers. In mediæval times this fateful law was referred to as the baleful influence of the stars. What other meaning could the mystic movements of these dim lamps have than the weaving of the destiny of man? In the ancient world weaknesses and fierce propensities to evil were the judgments of God, sent upon the children for the sins of the fathers. This idea received increased emphasis and justification from the prevalent notions of the submergence of the individual in the family and state. The rights of the person are of modern growth. In classic days he was inextricably bound in national and social connections. His ancestors' sins were his. That he actually bore the results in his own fortunes was an easily observed fact; that this was right the dominating social theories of the time maintained. In Hebrew literature this indissoluble connection between the generations found monumental utterance in the words: "For I the Lord thy God am a jealous God, visiting the iniquity of the fathers upon the children unto the third and fourth generation of them that hate me."

The aspect of hereditary evil which engaged Æschylus' attention was not that which would engross a modern writer, its deteriorating effects on the character of the offender. Neither was it the essential guilt of the sin itself. The Greek mind saw the horror of sin in its social results. Individual transgression called down the retributive justice of God, not merely upon the criminal, but upon the family and state. It blights the coming generations; it spreads its contagion beyond the wrong-doer.

To reveal the hereditary curse of sin by tracing its destructive course down through the house of Atreus is evidently a main purpose with Æschylus. When Cassandra, led as Agamemnon's captive, approaches the palace, her clairvoyant soul feels the chill horror of the doom which hangs over the place. Furies seem to possess the mansion, —

> "and in horrid measures chant
> The first base deed; recording with abhorrence
> Th' adulterous lust that stained a brother's bed."[1]

Of this same ancestral shadow the chorus speaks in stately measure in the "Libation-Pourers:" —

> "Alas, the inborn curse that haunts our house,
> Of Atè's blood-stained scourge the tuneless sound!
> Alas, the deep, insufferable doom,
> The staunchless wound!"[2]

Yet this "insufferable doom" is not something fickle and capricious; it is a well understood law of nature.

> "One base deed, with prolific power,
> Like its cursed stock engenders more;
> But to the just, with blooming grace,
> Still flourishes a beauteous race."[3]

[1] Potter's trans.   [2] Morshead's trans.   [3] Potter's trans.

The fierce, lawless blood of Atreus, who was willing to serve to his brother the horrid stew of his own children's limbs, transmitted to posterity, could not fail to break forth in dreadful crimes.

But although Æschylus represents this law of ancestral evil as working with the inevitableness of Fate, he never trespassed upon the domain of man's individual freedom. The wrath of the gods does not fall upon the devoted person until he has himself committed a sin which lets loose the impending avalanche. In some act of freedom he identifies himself with the guilt of his ancestors before he is swept into the black stream of inherited doom. It was when Agamemnon killed the sacred stag of Artemis and insolently boasted that he was the better hunter that the woe fell on him, —

"for his injurious pride
Filled for this house the cup of desolation
Fated himself to drain it to the dregs."[1]

"By my choice, my choice,
I freely sinned" [exclaims Prometheus].
"Because I gave
Honour to mortals, I have yoked my soul
To this compelling fate."[2]

The other formative thought of the "Oresteia" is the retributive judgments of God as seen in history. Sin cannot be confined to the one guilty; it goes down through the generations; it also

[1] Potter's trans.
[2] *Prometheus Bound*, E. B. Browning's trans.

sweeps in devastating circles out into the world. The whole Trojan war was caused by sin, and thus becomes an illustration of divine justice. Paris violated the laws of hospitality and carried Helen in triumph to Troy. No evil at first seemed to result. No keen-eyed justice seemed to observe the crime.

> "To Ilion's towers in wanton state
> With speed she wings her easy way;
> Soft gales obedient round her wait,
> And pant on the delighted sea."[1]

Yet God is not mocked; vengeance soon awakes.

> "But, such the doom of Jove,
> Vindictive round her nuptial bed,
> With threat'ning mien and footstep dread,
> Rushes, to Priam and his state severe,
> To rend the bleeding heart his stern delight,
> And from the bridal eye to force the tear,
> Erinnys, rising from the realms of night."[2]

But Æschylus traces this retributive justice to a finer issue than the strife of nations. In the ancient world the family and state were the two most important institutions. Each had its rights and each its limitations. Because each was limited it was partial, and being partial it was blind, and being blind it stumbled across its boundaries and trenched on the rights of the other. With each infringement of right there was an inevitable retribution, an expiatory penalty, which to Æschylus was a powerful witness to the sleepless vigilance and the minutely exacting justice of

[1] Potter's trans.   [2] Potter's trans.

God. Although Agamemnon is a great king, dignified, humble-minded, clear-seeing, powerful on the field and at the council board, and ever ready to subject all personal desires to the demands of his office, yet for his slight sin at Aulis he must sacrifice his daughter Iphigenia. A King's stern duty to avert the wrath of the gods, so that the expedition against Troy may proceed, compels him to make the dreadful offering. But in slaying his tearful, pleading daughter, while he has propitiated the gods, he has sinned against the family. These rights are also sacred, and this violation demands an adequate expiation. In the person of Clytemnestra the avenging justice of the home secures its satisfaction, and the victorious king returning to his violated hearth is slain in his bath. While securing justice for itself, the family has sinned against the state by killing the king, so that although the curtain may fall upon the "Agamemnon" when the king's crime has been expiated, it must rise upon the "Libation-Pourers" to show how the new offense has its atonement. In this second play Orestes, the prince, returns and at the bidding of Apollo slays his mother, who thus by her own death expiates the crime of murdering her husband. Again the curtain may fall, for justice has been done. Yet a new crime, as horrible as the others, has been perpetrated, — a son has reddened his hand in his mother's blood, and even though he did it at the command of a god and in the interests of justice, such an act of violence must meet with a fierce recoil. In the " Eumenides " the furies of a murdered mother pursue the frenzied Orestes even to the altar of Pallas, where he goes at the command of Phœbus. Here the prince pleads the justice of his cause, and the Erinnyes assert their rights, Pallas restores the equilibrium of the moral order and stays the havoc of the crime whose curse has passed from father to son by acquitting Orestes and bestowing extraordinary honor upon the Erinnyes. The sin has been expiated because its penalties have fallen upon a righteous man, and justice is appeased when its majesty is maintained.

We now see clearly the structual thoughts of this mighty trilogy. The Supreme Righteousness, whose highest manifestation is called Zeus, wise, beneficent, scrupulously just, foreordains all things. Yet sin is of human volition. Not until man takes the first wrong step does he link himself to his dreadful fate. Each sin is surely punished.

"It is well of these tales to tell ; for the sword in the grasp of the Right
With a cleaving, a piercing blow to the innermost heart doth smite,
And the deed unlawfully done is not trodden down nor forgot,
When the sinner outsteppeth the law and heedeth the high God not ;
But justice hath planted the anvil, and destiny forgeth the sword

That shall smite in her chosen time; by her is the child restored;
And, darkly devising, the Fiend of the house, world-cursed, will repay
The price of the blood of that slain, that was shed in a bygone day." [1]

Each slightest sin must be expiated.

" Blood for blood, and blow for blow —
Thou shalt reap as thou dost sow;
Age to age with hoary wisdom
Speaketh thus to man." [2]

"'T is robber robbed, and slayer slain; for though
Ofttimes it lag, with measured blow for blow,
Vengeance prevaileth
While great Jove lives. Who breaks the close-linked woe
Which heaven entaileth?" [3]

The inexorable Righteousness manifests itself by visiting the iniquity of the fathers upon the children unto the third and fourth generation, and by the retributive processes of history. Sin, therefore, in the teaching of Æschylus has a twofold aspect. It entails hereditary evil and embroils institutions and nations. If man were simply a member of a family, personal and hereditary suffering would end the consequences of transgression; but he is a citizen, a representative of a nation, and his actions may involve states and races unconnected by ties of blood.

How shall the hereditary and social curse of

---

[1] The *Libation-Pourers*, Morshead's trans.
[2] The *Libation-Pourers*, Blackie's trans.
[3] *Agamemnon*, Blackie's trans.

sin be stayed? How shall the divine justice be satisfied?

The hereditary blight is stayed when its penalties fall upon a righteous man. Orestes had not identified himself with the bad blood of his house. He had acted under a sense of duty, with perfect self-control and in obedience to the command of Apollo. Whatever stain there was upon him — and the murder of his mother made him guilty of a sin against the home — was washed away by his pains and lustrations, and when after many wanderings he came to the temple of Pallas Athene for justification he pleaded: —

> "No guilt of blood
> Is on my soul, nor is my hand unclean." [1]

The forensic justification came when a jury of Athenians and Pallas, representing human and divine justice, declared him innocent, and the Erinnyes were appeased by having suitable honors paid to them. His justification is based on his rectitude, his obedience to the divine commands, his sufferings and lustrations, together with the honors rendered to the Erinnyes. By these the majesty of the divine government has been sufficiently upheld to allow Orestes to go free.

The curse, so far as it affects one's judicial standing before God, having been allayed, how is the tainted blood purified? This hereditary evil that has broken out in so many directions, how is it

[1] *Eumenides*, Plumptre's trans.

checked? By the moral will of a good man. Orestes inherited murderous, passionate blood from both sides of his house, but he held it in subjection. In his freedom he yielded only to high motives, he carefully obeyed the will of the gods; and under this severe self-control the hot blood cooled, the evil was overcome by good. That the solution of Æschylus is right is a matter of daily observation. Man inherits from God as well as from the brute. The old conflict of St. Michael and the Dragon is reënacted in many breasts with the same results. The ape and the tiger die, and the good wins a lasting victory.

The vicarious suffering of a good man is efficacious also in staying the clash between the family and the state. Orestes is prince as well as son. He represents both the institutions which have been wronged by the havoc of Agamemnon's sin. In him they both can be reconciled. His righteousness honors both institutions and maintains their majesty unimpaired. There can be perfect divine forgiveness because hereditary evil has been overcome in a good man, because, being also representative of all the interests injured, he reconciles them in himself, and because his suffering righteousness and the homage paid to the messengers of justice maintain the authority of the divine law. In making a righteous man staunch the wound made by sin, Æschylus is not indulging in a passing fancy. With him this is a settled principle. When Prometheus is bound to the rocks because of his defiance of Zeus, Hermes says to him: —

> "Do not look
> For any end moreover to this curse,
> Or ere some god appear to accept thy pangs
> On his own head vicarious, and descend
> With unreluctant step the darks of hell
> And gloomy abysses around Tartarus."[1]

One cannot read these lines, written four hundred years before Calvary, without thinking of the vicarious Sufferer who being righteous tasted death for every man.

[1] *Prometheus Bound*, E. B. Browning's trans.

V

SOPHOCLES

Grant me henceforth, ye powers divine,
  In virtue's purest paths to tread!
  In every word, in every deed,
May sanctity of manners ever shine!
  Obedient to the laws of Jove,
  The laws descended from above,
Which, not like those by feeble mortals given,
  Buried in dark oblivion lie,
  Or worn by time decay, and die,
But bloom eternal like their native heaven!
                                    SOPHOCLES.

CHAPTER V

SOPHOCLES

From Æschylus the crown of tragic poetry passed to a man scarcely less smitten with a sense of the august grandeur of the moral law, and far more richly gifted in ability to analyze character and to delineate human passions. While Æschylus was absorbed in gazing at those unseen, invincible powers working so steadily for righteousness that man seemed scarcely more than a puppet in their hands, Sophocles turned his eyes to the deep places of the heart, and with unrivaled skill portrayed the struggles of the inner life. He was the Shakespeare of the ancient stage, broad in his sympathies, human in his interests, and unexcelled in the portrayal of the passions of the heart. Of the hundred plays which he wrote only seven have come down to us. In them we find uttered with impressive power the same essential truths of the inviolability of the moral law, and the sure recoil of evil upon the guilty, which were the inspiration of the masterpieces of his predecessor. In "Trachiniæ," "Philoctetes," "Ajax," "Electra," "Antigone" we find the same collision between different rights, — involving the same action and interaction of guilt and penalty, until at last the offended rights are expiated and find their common peace in the Right. We shall dwell upon only two of the plays, "Œdipus Tyrannus" and "Œdipus Coloneus," because in them the additional truth is emphasized that blunders are as disastrous as crimes, and that a mistake may disturb the moral order as violently as a great sin. It is the teaching of Sophocles concerning the expiation demanded by eternal righteousness from the unintentional offender, and the ways in which this sure justice atones to the blunderer for his awful sufferings, that give to these dramas their strange fascination.

The familiar yet always pathetic story of Œdipus runs as follows: Laius, king of Thebes, has been forewarned by the oracle that he will die by the hand of his own son. When his wife, Jocasta, gave birth to a boy, the alarmed king pierced the child's feet, bound them with thongs, and exposed him on Mt. Cithærus. Having been found by a shepherd of the king of Corinth, Œdipus was brought up in the palace as the king's son. Learning from an oracle that he was doomed to slay his father and marry his mother, he fled from the home of his shepherd father and mother, that he might be guiltless of the dreadful crime. On the road between Delphi and

Daulis the wanderer met his real father, Laius, and in a quarrel unintentionally slew him. Coming to Thebes, he found that devoted city plagued by the Sphinx, who, seated upon a rock in the neighborhood, propounded a riddle to every Theban passing by, and if the traveler could not answer it, killed him. Œdipus solved the riddle, and the Sphinx destroyed herself. For his reward he received the kingdom and the hand of the queen, Jocasta, in marriage. Thus while seeking with all his heart to avoid evil and serve his fellows, his very efforts to escape have made him the slayer of his father and the incestuous husband of his mother. Yet a guiltless blunder may be as morally disastrous as a deliberate offense. There is evil in the city and a plague falls upon it, destroying the fruits of the earth, the cattle of the fields, and the race of men, causing Hades to enlarge her borders. Œdipus, ignorant of his mistake, assures the terror-stricken people of his sympathy and pronounces a solemn curse upon the murderer, dooming him to exile when he is found. In his energetic endeavor to ferret him out he learns, to his utter horror, that he himself is the blood-stained criminal,—that he is a guilty parricide and the husband of his mother. Jocasta, overwhelmed by the awful truth, commits suicide to expiate her crime; but the agonized Œdipus realized that death would be no release and no atonement.

> "Descending to the dead, I know not how
> I could have borne to gaze upon my sire,
> Or my unhappy mother; for to them
> Crimes dark as mine not death can e'er atone."

Over the dead body of his mother he tears out his eyes that they may not see his sufferings and the dreadful deeds he has wrought. Then he goes forth from the country a homeless exile.

In recounting this frightful tale Sophocles is too skillful an artist to make it one of unmitigated horror. He shows that Œdipus is not entirely undeserving of his punishment. Prosperity has to a degree hardened his heart, making him imperious and headstrong, so that his sufferings are not simply the fierce scourgings of Fate, but minister to his final perfection.

When the curtain falls we have beheld a noble man, through his blunders enmeshed in the toils of retributive justice, in his very efforts to do good sinking deeper into the net, and by his unavoidable mistakes bringing fiery disaster to those whom he would help.

Yet the gods are just. The punishment has been greater than the guilt, and even if the recoil against evil was inevitable, the blow that fell upon the unintentional offender was heavier than he deserved. The gods must atone to Œdipus for the severity of the penalty. Justice must be done to him, and the "Œdipus Tyrannus" must be followed by "Œdipus Coloneus."

Between "Œdipus Tyrannus" and "Œdipus Coloneus" several years have elapsed. The blind and fallen king, now an old man, broken and worn by his sufferings, comes as a suppliant to Athens. The wrath of an avenging righteous order has been appeased by his grievous woes, and the time has come for reconciliation and peace. Œdipus has been the cause of frightful evils, and he has atoned for them by sufferings worse than death. Yet although the source of wrong, he has acted in the innocency of his heart; the retributions he has endured are out of all proportion to his guilt; the gods are in his debt and must do him justice. They do this by giving him double for what he has lost. He had been driven from Theban soil; Creon beseeches him to return. He had been deprived of his power; Fate now gives him the authority to determine who shall occupy his throne. Polynices, his son, comes pleading his father's forgiveness and asking for a blessing upon his arms. He is dismissed with an awful curse. Theseus, the hero king of Athens, welcomes him with great honor and promises him full protection. But supernatural glories await the one who has so nobly borne the inflictions of divine justice. Jove's thunders peal fearfully overhead, and all are awed before this dread person whom the gods are about signally to honor. In one of the finest passages in ancient literature the story is told of how Œdipus, to prepare himself for his translation, washed himself in pure water, put on a spotless garment, and, summoned by the thunders of Zeus, bade his faithful daughters an affectionate farewell. After a brief silence a voice is heard calling Œdipus to hasten his departure. The awe-stricken attendants now hurry away, leaving the one about to be glorified in the company of the Athenian king. When the affrighted followers had sufficiently recovered from their superstitious terror to look back, they were amazed to see the king standing alone, covering his eyes with his hand to shut out a sight too glorious for mortal vision to behold. Thus by the apotheosis of Œdipus did the gods at last adjust the scales.

With almost preternatural power Sophocles has dealt with the problem of sin, retribution, and reconciliation. Sin is the transgression of the law. It have may been committed unconsciously, yet it unlooses the terrible forces of retribution. This is not a poet's dream or a pagan superstition. No law can be violated with impunity, even though the offender acts in ignorance. Retribution for every offense is seen to be swift, sure, overwhelming. Reconciliation is treated only in the one aspect of expiation.

Sophocles was a deeply religious man. His constant theme is reverence for God. Partly in deference to popular superstition, partly for its convenience in symbolizing local manifestation of the divine power, he made use of polytheism, but his religion is essentially monotheistic. There is one unchangeable divine order; one inexorable, mysterious, irresistible Will who decrees the fate of mortals and sends his sure judgment against iniquity. If a man sins, the penalty is upon him and upon his children even to the third and fourth generation. Through his prophets God foretells the doom of the fated house. In vain one seeks to avert the impending calamity. No wiles nor tricks can turn aside the inevitable decrees. Yet they do not fall upon one perfectly righteous. Against the throne where justice sits on high man stumbles. Some act of pride, some moment of self-will, some outburst of impetuous temper identifies the victim with the sin of his house, and then upon him the avalanche of woe falls. This is simply a dramatic interpretation of the laws of heredity, or of the will of God. When powerfully and concretely visualized it shocks us and we think it a pagan view of life, but Sophocles is simply describing certain familiar laws which we believe are the expression of the will of the Eternal Righteousness.

Of the inviolability of the Right, Sophocles had no doubt. God—

> "never yet to human wrong
> Left the unbalanc'd scale."

Penalty is always exacted. It is an eye for an eye and a tooth for a tooth. God is not mocked;

each must reap his harvest. There is no atonement, no reconciliation with God, until justice has been done. What will satisfy divine justice? What will expiate sin? The answer we find in Œdipus is that it is suffering endured submissively until the heart is purified and the will subdued. Sufferings thus borne propitiate the moral indignation both of the gods and man. If Œdipus had shown no sense of the greatness of his offenses and had lived in ease and power, utterly ignoring them, we can conceive that then there would have been an outburst in Thebes and from the oracles, which would have brought him to a consciousness of his misdeeds. But knowing his sin, repenting of it, and suffering for it, he expiated it.

Sophocles does not work out the whole problem of reconciliation. The curse does not stop with Œdipus, else we should not have had Antigone's sufferings in later years. With his confidence in heaven's regard, his knowledge that retribution will overtake his enemies, his assurance that mighty in his grave he will prove a blessing to the land which sheltered him, and that evil has worked good, Œdipus is partially reconciled to his fate. But although our problem is only partially solved, we have learned enough to feel that in our interpretation of the atonement we must not slur over those principles of righteousness which Sophocles has so powerfully expounded.

VI

DANTE

The Divina Commedia is one of the landmarks of history. More than a magnificent poem, more than the beginning of a language and the opening of a national literature, more than the inspirer of art, and the glory of a great people, it is one of those rare and solemn monuments of the mind's power, which measure and test what it can reach to, which rise up ineffaceably and forever as time goes on, marking out its advance by grander divisions than its centuries, and adopted as epochs by the consent of all who come after. It stands with the Iliad and Shakespeare's plays, with the writings of Aristotle and Plato, with the Novum Organon and the Principia, with Justin's Code, and with the Parthenon and St. Peter's. It is the first Christian poem; and it opens European literature, as the Iliad did that of Greece and Rome. And, like the Iliad, it has never become out of date; it accompanies in undiminished freshness the literature which it began.

DEAN CHURCH.

CHAPTER VI

DANTE

THE next writer of permanent and commanding fame who can help us in our investigation is Dante. That we pass immediately from Athens to Florence will doubtless surprise the reader. Latin literature would naturally engage our attention, Rome succeeding Athens as the centre of the world's intellectual leadership. But the Roman mind sadly lacked in ethical and spiritual originality. Executive force, and not the open vision into the world of spiritual realities, was the glory of the Eternal City. Rome was an unblushing borrower. Greek plays were put upon the stage and received with enthusiasm, but in all the centuries of Roman dominion there arose no dramatist, no poet, no spiritual genius of any kind who dealt, even in a second-rate manner, with the theme which has been organic in all other great literatures. It seems strange that the world's most massive civilization rose and crumbled without having a single soul break away from the dead level of the national genius, and utter a clear and original word on the existence and healing of the great discord. Over a monotonous and, for our present purpose, a spiritual desert, we fly until we come to the "poet saturnine."

Sin, Retribution, Reconciliation, are preëminently his theme. Like Homer he represents more than himself: he is the voice of a distinct epoch of thought. He does not utter his individual conclusions, but sets forth in forms of imperishable beauty the subtly analyzed experiences and the matured convictions of many generations. What the Christian world during ten centuries had, by earnest battles with formidable difficulties, learned the significance of life to be, what it sought after with passionate aspirations and dreaded with superstitious fears, what profound and clear-visioned men had wrought into doctrine, — all this Thomas Aquinas concatenated in his "Summa Theologica" into a minute and marvelously comprehensive system of thought; and this Dante made immortal by the music of his verse and the vividness of his pictures. The evidential value of the poet's testimony is greater than if he gave simply the insights of his genius. He speaks for the accumulated experience and faith of a thousand years. His voice is the voice of many waters.

It becomes us to beware of a certain modern superciliousness toward mediæval thought as semi-barbarous and ignorant. The spiritual needs of men do not differ much from age to age. Forms of expression change, but the generations face the same mysteries, bear the same burdens, and feel the same hungerings and thirstings. Wisdom in things spiritual is not dependent on breadth of scientific knowledge, else Moses, Isaiah, and Paul would be blind guides. The world has known no more astute, profound, and saintly minds than those who brought forth the mediæval conception of the relation of God to the soul. We may employ different symbols and occupy a different point of view, but the truth which gave to their characters enduring strength and saintly beauty is still vital.

The mediæval world is so opposite to our own that it is easier to understand the Greek dramatists and even Homer than it is to comprehend the great Florentine, yet Dante is not obscure in his essential teachings. "Midway upon the journey of our life," he tells us in the "Divine Comedy," "I found myself within a dark wood, for the right way had been missed. Ah! how hard a thing it is to tell what this wild and rough and dense wood was, which in thought renews the fear! So bitter is it that death is little more. But in order to treat of the good that there I found, I will tell of the other things that I have seen there. I cannot well recount how I entered it, so full was I of slumber at that point where I abandoned the true way. But after I had arrived at the foot of a hill, where that valley ended which had pierced my heart with fear, I looked on high, and saw its shoulders clothed already with the rays of the planet that leadeth men aright along every path." He essayed to climb this sunlit mountain, but three wild beasts sprang out upon him,— a she-leopard, a lion, and a she-wolf. Dante fought valiantly against them for a time, but little by little they pushed him back to where "the Sun is silent." "While I was falling back to the low place, before mine eyes appeared one who through long silence seemed hoarse. When I saw him in the great desert, 'Have pity on me!' I cried to him, 'whatso thou art, or shade or real man.'"[1] It was Virgil who promised to lead him in a better way.

Dante intimates in this beautiful symbolism that when he was thirty-five years of age he awoke to find that he had missed the way of true life. Seeing before him the sunlit mountain of virtue, he tried to climb it with no strength save his own unaided powers, but the sins of incontinence, violence, and fraud were too strong for him. Then Reason came to reveal the true path to blessedness. The "Divine Comedy" is Dante's interpretation of the way of life. Reason, symbolized by Virgil, shows him in the "Inferno" what is the real nature of sin and its dreadful consequences. In the "Purgatorio" is disclosed how the stain

[1] All the quotations in this chapter are from Charles Eliot Norton's translation of the "Divine Comedy."

of sin is expunged from the soul. Beyond this, Reason, even though enlightened by divine grace, cannot go, and a new guide, Beatrice, type of the Divine Revelation, leads the eager, purified soul into the celestial mysteries, until by direct vision Dante sees God face to face.

On no page in literature are the facts of sin and retribution and the processes of reconciliation more thoroughly considered or more powerfully explained than in the "Divine Comedy."

The "Inferno" is not a description of a prison house of torture, but is a descent into human experience. It is the poet's declaration of the character of sin. Dante seems to have said within himself, "Let the theologians wrangle about their definitions; their contentions issue in nothing. I will portray sin in colors so lurid and in figures so hideous that men will see its true nature, — see it so vividly that they will turn back their feet from the way of death!" This could be done only by painting sin in its ultimate conditions when it is stripped of all blandishments and has brought forth its full fruition. The "Inferno," therefore, is to be read as Dante's conception of sin and retribution. He employs three distinct ways of enforcing his thought.

Sin is symbolized in the repulsive monsters presiding over the concentric circles. In them sin is declared to be vulgar, brutal, grotesque.

The environment also suggests the nature of

the evil there requited. The incontinent are punished in a zone of darkness, for this sin extinguishes the light of the mind. The violent in a zone of fire learn that God is a consuming flame against the rebellious. The lowest pit is a zone of arctic cold, for the soul is in its deepest hell when its sympathies are congealed, its sensibilities are extinct, and the whole nature dead in sin.

The method of punishment discloses even more elaborately Dante's thought. The lustful are swept about on a never-resting storm; hypocrites wear a leaden cloak that looks like gold; flatterers wallow in filth.

But it is in the person and condition of Lucifer that the poet most powerfully delineates his vision of sin. At the bottom of the pit, and therefore at the point farthest removed from God, is his prison house. Huge, bloody, loathsome, grotesque, self-absorbed; not dead nor yet alive; having three faces, one fiery red, one between white and yellow, one black, — indicating the threefold character of sin as malignant, impotent, and ignorant, — every moment sending forth chilling death, making others woeful in his own woes, punishing his followers with frightful torture, and undoing himself; the tears of the world flowing back to him as their source and becoming his torment; the movement of his wings, by which he seeks to extricate himself, freezing the rivers of tears and blood and thus imprisoning him, — what more fitting personification could this seer have devised to show evil in its real deformity and folly? The unsightly and self-centred Lucifer is perhaps the truest characterization of sin in literature.

The retributions of wrong-doing are sure and terrible. The real penalty of sin is not so much what happens to a man as what takes place within him. The sinner's emotions and deeds fashion the character in which we must live. There is no evading the reprisals of wrong-doing. Instantly the effect is registered upon the soul of the perpetrator.

The feature which most impressed Dante, as it did Homer, was the blindness with which the sinner was smitten. As they entered the dreadful portal of the lower world, Virgil said to his companion: "We have come to the place where I have told thee that thou shalt see the woeful people, who have lost the good of the understanding." In the poet's philosophy the *summum bonum* is to see God's power in nature, and his justice and love in individual and national life; to behold only unconscious force in nature, and pitiless fate and capricious chance in human affairs, is the earth's Inferno. This penal blindness, which by unwearied law the Most High dispenses to lawless desires, is sin's most dreadful consequence.

Dante agrees with the other authors whom we have studied, that we come to a knowledge of sin by the shock of its results, only he does not trace it in the curse smiting a family, or in a plague devastating a city, but in the blindness, torture, and sterility of the sinner's own soul.

The problem of Reconciliation Dante works out in the "Purgatorio" in a way most impressive. Although, contrary to the common impression, he centres his theology in the love of God, believing that the unspeakable glory of that love, flashing down through the various spheres, penetrates all things; yet as the divinely appointed prophet of the exactitude and majesty of the moral law, he asserts that before the soul can be freed from the bondage of sin there are certain inexorable, judicial requirements which must be met. He accepted the prevalent notion of his time that Christ's death on the cross was a satisfaction to divine justice, remitting the eternal penalties of sin to all who by baptism and repentance identified themselves with the Son of God. What man must do to complete the reconciliation he shows most vividly and minutely as he makes the ascent of the Purgatorial mountain. This teaching is epitomized in a single picture of great power and suggestiveness: Following Virgil he moves to a cliff which rises sheer before him, where in a rift, he says, " I saw a gate, and three steps beneath for going to it of divers colors, and a gate-keeper who as yet said not a word. . . . Thither we came to the first great stair; it was of white marble so polished and smooth that I mirrored myself in it as I appear. The second, of deeper hue than perse, was of a rough and scorched stone, cracked lengthwise and athwart. The third, which above lies massy, seemed to me of porphyry as flaming red as blood that spirts forth from a vein. Upon this the Angel of God held both his feet, sitting upon the threshold that seemed to me stone of adamant. Up over the three steps my Leader drew me with good will, saying, 'Beg humbly that he undo the lock.' Devoutly I threw myself at the holy feet; I besought for mercy's sake that he would open for me; but first upon my breast I struck three times. Seven P's upon my forehead he inscribed with the point of his sword, and 'See that thou wash these wounds when thou art within,' he said." [1]

The gate symbolizes justification. Ere a man can be justified before God he must know his sin, seeing himself mirrored exactly as he is; he must repent of it, and render full satisfaction for it. There are three steps, confession, contrition, satisfaction, declared by the Catholic Church to be necessary for justification. Confession is not mere verbal acknowledgment. It is a self-mirroring, so that the soul stands before itself and the world in its true light. Contrition

[1] *Purgatorio*, ix, 94–114.

must be absolute and sincere, and the satisfaction rendered to God is the work of Christ, supplemented by the sinner's own expiatory deeds. The seven P's — *Peccata* — signify the seven mortal sins which must be purged away before the stained soul is pure in the sight of God. Passing through the gate of justification, Dante traversed the seven ledges of the Holy Mountain. Upon each he learns how the scum of one of the seven mortal sins is dissolved from off the conscience, and the primitive lustre is restored. The penitent spirits are taught fully to understand the nature of their sin and of the contrary virtue, and are persuaded to practice that virtue so as both to satisfy divine justice and to heal the wounds sin has made in the soul. When confession, contrition, and satisfaction effect their perfect work all vestiges of sin are obliterated from the chastened spirit. He is now at the top of the mountain, and has reached the moral condition of the first man. This is indicated by Virgil's triumphant words: "Free, upright, and sound is thine own will, and it would be wrong not to act according to its choice; wherefore thee over thyself I crown and mitre."[1]

There is one phase of reconciliation which we meet with for the first time. It was hinted at by Sophocles when Œdipus, the moment after he has torn out his eyes, exclaims: —

[1] *Purgatorio*, xxvii, 140-142.

"More painful is the memory of my crimes
Than all the wounds my wild distractions made."

The thought is not taken up again, and we can only surmise that the painful memory was healed by the balm of time and the consciousness of the power and blessedness which were to be his through the special honor of Zeus. But Dante soberly faces the problem of an atonement for the memory. There is no perfect reconciliation unless one is reconciled to his past. He cannot carry a memory ashamed and embittered into the bliss of the next world. It would be a dark spot amid supernal glory, a drop of poison in the cup of life, a discord amid celestial harmonies. It is not enough for God to forgive the sinner; the contrite one must so view his past that he can forgive himself. In one of the most beautiful passages in literature Dante describes this experience.[1] The seven P's had been cleansed from his forehead, and the stains of the seven mortal sins from his soul. He had met Beatrice and confessed his unfaithfulness, yet he cannot enter celestial joys with a befouled memory. Then it was that Matilda, type of a life of virtuous activity, "drew me into the stream up to the throat, and dragging me after her was moving over the water light as a shuttle. When I was near the blessed shore, I heard 'Asperges me' so sweetly that I cannot remember it, far less write

[1] *Purgatorio*, xxxi.

it. The beautiful lady opened her arms, clasped my head, and plunged me in where I had perforce to swallow of the water." In the dark waters of Lethe, which flows out of the fountain of the grace of God, all memory of sin vanished to trouble him no more.

One should hesitate long before criticising a great experience so beautifully delineated, yet a Lethe which thoroughly washed away all the foul blots from our memories and left merely the recollection of the good would deprive us of a large part of our richest heritage. Only a mangled, half-instructed creature would remain. We need the background of our whole past if we are to understand its significance and wisely meet the future. Moreover, a life of virtuous activity cannot so immerse us in a stream of events that an evil past will cease to trouble us. Dante's vision, at the close of the "Paradiso," of all things held in the light and love of God, furnishes a better solution of the problem of a blackened memory than his Lethe. A disagreeable past is more satisfactorily disposed of when it is seen immersed in the Lake of Sempiternal Light, than when allowed to float down the dark stream of forgetfulness.

One further experience the poet passes through in his reconciliation with his past. Following his gentle guide, he enters the river Eunoë, a creation of his own imagination, whose draught was so sweet that it could never have sated him. Thus does he symbolize that there is an energy working in a redeemed spirit which recreates it, and gives it complete victory over the effects of sin.

While the "Purgatorio" teaches that confession, contrition, and satisfaction, which heal the hurts of sin and restore our nature to its original freedom, are the first steps in religion, the methods by which the full joy of reconciliation are reached are described in the "Paradiso." Fixing his eyes upon Beatrice — symbol of the Revealed Truth of God — with that look of faith which is the soul's intuitive and final abandonment of itself to another, Dante ascends from star to star, from virtue to virtue, until, perfected in character, he is capable of enjoying the ultimate blessedness. Led on by St. Bernard, the exponent of mystic faith, he approaches the Fountain of Living Light Eternal. With anointed eyes he looks.

"My sight, becoming pure, was entering more and more through the radiance of the lofty Light which of itself is true. I saw that in its depths is enclosed, bound up with love in one volume, that which is dispersed in leaves through the universe; substance and accidents and their modes fused together, as it were, in such wise that that of which I speak is one simple Light. In that Light one becomes such that it is impossible he should ever consent to turn himself from it for other sight; because the Good which is the object of the will is all collected in it, and outside of it that is defective which is perfect there. Within the profound and clear subsistence of the lofty Light appeared to me three circles of three colors and of one dimension; and one seemed reflected by the other, as Iris by Iris, and the third seemed fire which from the one and from the other is equally breathed forth. That circle, which appeared in Thee generated as a reflected light, being awhile surveyed by my eyes, seemed to me depicted with our effigy within itself, of its own very color, wherefore my sight was wholly set upon it. As is the geometer who wholly applies himself to measure the circle, and finds not by thinking that principle of which he is in need, such was I at that new sight. I wished to see how the image was conformed to the circle, and how it has its place therein; but my own wings were not for this, had it not been that my mind was smitten by a flash in which its wish came.

"To my high fantasy here power failed; but now my desire and my will were revolved, like a wheel which is moved evenly, by the Love which moves the sun and other stars."[1]

To see God in all things and all things in God, bound in one volume of love, and to know that God is in humanity and that our humanity is rooted and grounded in him, — this is life eternal; this is perfect reconciliation.

[1] *Paradiso,* xxxiii.

In reflecting upon the principles which Dante — or rather the Middle Ages speaking through him — considered essential to reconciliation, it is extremely interesting to note that every principle recognized by the authors we have studied is distinctly stated by him, while some which they dimly apprehended he clearly enunciates. With Homer, Æschylus, Sophocles, he emphasizes the defilement of sin, only he paints it more minutely and powerfully. What in Homer is a mere ceremonial pollution in Dante is distortion of soul. This is his constant thought in every circle of Hell, and on every ledge of Purgatory. Even by looking upon sin in his descent through the gulf of the infernal regions there is grime on his face which Virgil washes off with the dew. With Sophocles, he points out the necessity of the sinner seeing himself mirrored as he is, and the need of being truly contrite.

His reverence for the sanctity and integrity of the moral universe is as exalted as theirs. The blood-red step of satisfaction is with him, as with them, the final and inevitable step. 'No writer of ancient or modern times puts more insistent emphasis on a full settlement with righteousness than this stern prophet of the justice of God. Sin is so destructive that it works havoc in a delicately adjusted moral system. "And to his dignity he [man] never returns, unless, where sin makes void, he fill up for evil pleasures with just penalties."[1] Although the arms of divine mercy are so wide extended, still God cannot receive the sinner to himself until the void has been filled. Christ, who is, like Orestes, the representative of both parties, by his death offers a satisfaction. He might have paid all the debt, but he lets man have some part in the work by enjoining upon him the expiation of all the temporal penalties of sin. How these sins are expiated is one of the prominent features of the "Purgatorio," and the necessity for rendering such satisfaction is constantly reiterated. On the ledge of Pride this is stated repeatedly: "And here must I bear this load for it till God be satisfied," "of such pride the fee is here paid," "such coin does every one pay in satisfaction."[2] The avaricious lie prostrate; "so long as it shall be the pleasure of the just Lord, so long shall we stay immovable and outstretched."[3] The gluttonous "go loosing the knot of their debt."[4] The lustful are in the flames because "with such cure it is needful, and with such diet, that the last wound of all should be closed up."[5] The expiatory penalties, however, are not vindictive or arbitrary, but are adjusted to the purification of the soul. They are both a satisfaction rendered to a violated moral order, and are remedial to the peni-

[1] *Paradiso*, vii, 82. [2] *Purgatorio*, xi, 70, 71, 88, 125.
[3] *Purgatorio*, xix, 125, 126. [4] *Purgatorio*, xxiii, 15.
[5] *Purgatorio*, xxv, 138, 139.

tent by confirming him in right habits of thought and action.

The void made by sin must be filled; complete reparation must be made; God must be just in the act of forgiveness; else the pillared firmament is rottenness, and earth's base built on stubble,— to this conviction Dante yielded no half-hearted assent.

His original contribution to our study is the clear recognition of what Sophocles dimly beheld, *viz.*, that man must be reconciled to his past. How this is done he partially answers in his symbol of Lethe, indicating that virtuous activity changes our relation to the past, making it an alien and forgotten thing, and at the same time, as the river Eunoë suggests, healing the wounds and overcoming the weaknesses caused by sin. The final and complete answer is in the ultimate vision, when he sees all things perfect in God, bound together in the one volume of his love. The guiltiest soul can look upon his record and still join in the full joys of redemption when through all his experiences he sees the glory of God's perfect justice and love.

Sophocles could not fully answer this question of peace for a tormenting memory, or depict an unshadowed reconciliation, because his unanointed eyes had not caught sight of the glory of the Christian revelation that in infinite love all things consist and in that love they shall finally be known. Therefore the apotheosis of Œdipus was his nearest approach. He recognized Dante's problem, and groped for the same answer, but he saw through a glass darkly.

Dante also adds to our thought something which is only faintly glimpsed in the authors we have considered, but which becomes more conspicuous in later writers. Men of to-day are not greatly concerned to secure pardon before a hypothetical judgment-seat of God; but they have many a bitter struggle to acquiesce in the providential order of the world, and the discipline God inflicts upon them. This new and important phase of reconciliation Dante recognizes and solves. He affirms that even though a man experiences the drenching gloom of hell, and feels the sting of purgatorial discipline, yet if his habitual moods are those of faith, hope, and love he will attain such a firm conviction of the Goodness penetrating all things that he will be joined to God in a rapturous reconciliation. He is able joyfully to accept life and all that it brings of weal or woe, so unshaken is his certitude of the Divine Compassion.

VII

SHAKESPEARE

Of this Shakespeare of ours, perhaps the one opinion one sometimes hears a little idolatrously expressed is, in fact, the right one; I think the best judgment not of this country only, but of Europe at large, is slowly pointing to the conclusion, that Shakespeare is the chief of all poets hitherto; the greatest intellect who, in our recorded world, has left record of himself in way of literature. On the whole, I know not such a power of vision, such faculty of thought, if we take all the characters of it, in any other man. Such a calmness of depth; placid joyous strength; all things imaged in that great soul of his so true and clear, as in a tranquil and unfathomable sea! — THOMAS CARLYLE.

CHAPTER VII

SHAKESPEARE

THE next mind to arrest our attention because of its depth of insight into the woes and victories of life is that of Shakespeare. His point of view is very different from Dante's. While Shakespeare is "world-wide" in his sympathies, he very clearly stands with the group of healthy, robust, thoroughly mundane poets of the Elizabethan era in his outlook upon humanity. It was a lusty, vigorous age, in which things temporal loomed large and seemed eminently worth while. Dante saw life *sub specie aeternitatis*. Shakespeare beheld the eternal only as it revealed itself under the conditions of time. Yet his was too deep a mind not to feel the encompassing, ever-present mystery into which all that is plain shades off. His emotions in the presence of the Unknown were those of Goethe, which Carlyle has so beautifully expressed: —

> "Stars silent rest o'er us,
> Graves under us silent,
> And while earnest thou gazest
> Comes boding of terror,
> Comes phantasm and error

> Perplexing the bravest
> With doubt and misgiving.
> But heard are the voices,
> Heard are the sages,
> The World and the Ages.
> Choose well, your choice is
> Brief but yet endless."

The positive religious note which Shakespeare strikes is the same as that which vibrated so powerfully in the Greek tragedies. The Englishman is even more impressive than they in the titanic energy with which he utters his judgment of sin and its entail of woe. His theology seems to resolve itself into the clear recognition of a Universal Law, inexorable, divinely ordained, manifested in the minutest actions of life and in the vast upheavals of society. In this closely woven, all-penetrating network of moral forces man has his being. He is free to do the one act which, once performed, involves him in the toils of the inevitable reaction. The recoil may be a just recompense for evil, as in the case of Macbeth, or it may pile up vicarious suffering for the innocent, as in the sorrows of Juliet. It is in this austere conception of a moral equilibrium disturbed by willful sin and foolish passion that Shakespeare's religious sentiments most powerfully disclose themselves.

Shakespeare's graphic portrayals of sin and its nemesis are so familiar that we shall not linger over them. Macbeth has his moment of freedom;

then, yielding to temptation, he is caught in the grip of Necessity, tormented by horror within and disorders without, until he dies a forsaken wretch in a losing battle. His "fiend-like queen" suffered similar torments, and "by self and violent hands took off her life."

In Richard III every movement of the play is the development of some phase of retribution. In that terrible scene [1] when Queen Margaret curses the various Yorkist conspirators, the spectator is made to feel that the woes about to light on the reigning house are punishments for crimes against the house of Lancaster, while Richard intimates that the wounds of Lancaster are requitals for deeds done to the house of York.

For Richard's heinous sins simple death on the battlefield, or by the hand of an assassin, is not penalty enough. His crimes have been too atrocious and multiplied. He is not only the tool of Providence working compensation upon others commensurate with their guilt; his preëminence in evil singles him out for conspicuous retribution. What this is to be Margaret foretells:—

> "The worm of conscience still be-gnaw thy soul!
> Thy friends suspect for traitors while thou liv'st,
> And take deep traitors for thy dearest friends!
> No sleep close up that deadly eye of thine,
> Unless it be while some tormenting dream
> Affrights thee with a hell of ugly devils!
> Thou elvish-mark'd, abortive, rooting hog!" [2]

---

[1] *Richard III*, Act I, sc. iii.   [2] Act I, sc. i.i.

This was fulfilled in the famous night scene, when, with his imperious will helpless in sleep, the frenzy of remorse holds its high carnival in his soul.

To cite additional instances proving that Shakespeare believed as firmly as did Dante, Sophocles, or Æschylus in the moral framework of the world, is certainly unnecessary.

In unraveling the net of evil and revealing the final reconciliation, the English dramatist gives us valuable help. The mind of the spectator, pained, thrilled, awed by the experiences passed through, must find rest at last in what is at least a partial satisfaction. Sometimes the victim triumphs over his foes and receives visible compensation for his losses, as when Prospero held his enemies in his power, forgave them, and received back his dukedom. But life usually offers no such easy solution. Evil is not fully punished, nor virtue rewarded, in our actual experience. Some hurts are too deep to be healed by any temporal prosperity. Satisfactions deeper than any worldly dignities can give are needed. To meet this demand for the Eternal to explain and readjust the entanglements of time, dramatists have had recourse to the great Reconciler, Death. Upon the stormy stage where passions have clashed and sin has displayed its dreadful hideousness, where guilt and innocence, blindness, folly, malignity, have struggled in feverish intensity, comes at last the repose and unconquerable peace of death. So often is death employed as the *dénouement* of tragedy, that tragedy and death have become synonymous. For the guilty soul, death with its awful mystery, its suggestion of a judgment to come where perfect equity will be meted out to all, affords not only a necessary artistic ending of the drama, but satisfies our instincts for justice. So Agamemnon, Jocasta, Macbeth, all expiate their crimes.

The innocent victim caught in the coil of evil finally passes to "where beyond these voices there is peace."

> "Duncan is in his grave:
> After life's fitful fever, he sleeps well."

The stately repose compensates for the fever. In the death of the innocent there is always a suggestion of eternal peace, of being beyond the raving and malice of foes, an intimation of a final vindication that reconciles the spectator to the fate of the guiltless victim. Often the dramatic artist feels that he must make it clear that death ushers in the final compensation, as when Sophocles surrounds the death of Œdipus with supernatural portents, or when Shakespeare makes Horatio exclaim over the dead Hamlet:

> " Good-night, sweet prince,
> And flights of angels sing thee to thy rest!"

or when Goethe represents a voice from heaven crying at Margaret's death, " Is saved."

But Shakespeare's mind could not permanently

be satisfied with such a conception of life as is revealed in the tragedies. Neither could he push the solution of life's dissonance over into the mysteries of that future existence of which death is the portal. He was too intensely human, too thoroughly interested in the life that now is, to lay great stress upon a possible adjustment beyond the veil. What forces of reconciliation are now active, making life endurable and of rich significance? A mind like his was too sane and had too much of rational joy in it to be content with such a picture of life as he had drawn in his darker moods, — Iago sitting cool and malignant, with Othello and Desdemona dead; Ophelia a suicide and Hamlet a corpse through another's sin; Cordelia's sweet spirit extinguished by a villain's hasty order, and Lear's choleric temper spreading a horrible devastation. Is evil supreme? Must men perish in their blindness? Is there no redeeming energy in the world that opens the eyes of the blind, breaks the hideous power of sin, and brings peace and wisdom out of discord? Shakespeare in his later plays seems to have sought a reconciliation with the world for his own soul's good, so that in these we find the interest centred in the study of the forces which knit up the raveled sleeve of life.

In 1610 he retired from the theatre and went to live in Stratford. In 1611, as nearly as the date can be fixed, we have two plays from his pen, "The Winter's Tale" and "The Tempest," both of them revealing the ways in which life's wounds are healed.

In "The Winter's Tale," Leontes, in a passion of inordinate and senseless jealousy, accuses his noble queen of infidelity. His frenzy is as overwhelming as that of Othello, but in this play it is met by a fortitude which Desdemona did not possess. Hermione girds herself for the ordeal:

> "There's some ill planet reigns;
> I must be patient till the heavens look
> With an aspect more favourable. Good my lords,
> I am not prone to weeping, as our sex
> Commonly are; the want of which vain dew
> Perchance shall dry your pities; but I have
> That honourable grief lodged here, which burns
> Worse than tears drown." [1]

She believes that her innocence will be established, and that her sufferings will work repentance in her husband's heart:—

> "How this will grieve you,
> When you shall come to clearer knowledge, that
> You have thus publish'd me!" [1]

Yet sin is no such light thing that confession can atone for it: —

> "Gentle my lord,
> You scarce can right me thoroughly then, to say
> You did mistake." [1]

When Leontes' sin bears fruit in the supposed death of Hermione and the death of his son, he immediately repents, and sets about repairing the

[1] Act I, sc. i.

damage of his fault. This, Paulina reminds him, is no easy task: —

> "But, O thou tyrant!
> Do not repent these things; for they are heavier
> Than all thy woes can stir; therefore betake thee
> To nothing but despair. A thousand knees
> Ten thousand years together, naked, fasting,
> Upon a barren mountain, and still winter
> In storm perpetual, could not move the gods
> To look that way thou wert."[1]

For sixteen years Leontes sought by prayer and good deeds to expiate his sin. Sorrow and remorse purge the evil from his nature, until the good queen, who has been in hiding while this cleansing, upbuilding process was going on, reveals herself, and in her silent embrace forgives the wretched past. The play further discloses how out of evil good comes, not only to the chastened nature of the king, but to his discarded daughter, Perdita. The teaching is clear that the evil-doer may be brought to repentance by patient goodness, cleansed by sorrow, and finally forgiven.

In "The Tempest" we have a more perfect development of the same theme. This is probably the last complete play the great dramatist wrote. He holds his wondrous Ariel for a few hours till his task is done, and then he sets him at liberty.

> "I'll break my staff,
> Bury it certain fathoms in the earth,
> And deeper than did ever plummet sound,
> I'll drown my book."[2]

[1] Act III, sc. ii.   [2] Act V, sc. i.

The poet's own final feeling toward life and its meaning is revealed in the mellow, kindly light which rests upon the whole scene. The play expresses also his mature convictions. In order that in the space of a few hours he may epitomize life, its constituent forces and ultimate issue, Shakespeare has recourse to enchantment; this gives the will of his hero unhindered sway, and enables him to mould all things to his purpose.

"The Tempest" mirrors not only Shakespeare's mind as he bids farewell to the stage; it also, as a necessary result, gives us his ideal character. If Henry V is the poet's ideal man of the world, Prospero is unquestionably his moral hero. Sane, efficient, irreproachable in moral elevation, yet having tenderest sympathies, he represents man at his best estate, the man our supreme poet himself would be.

But the conditions of the play carry us still further. Prospero on his enchanted island is omnipotent; all spirits and forces obey his will. He is in his domain what the Everlasting is amid his worlds. In delineating how an ideal man would behave toward his enemies Shakespeare has given us a clear glimpse of his conception of the character of the Divinity that shapes our ends. For our study, therefore, "The Tempest" is invaluable. It gives us Shakespeare's idea of an overruling Providence in its relation to sin, and makes known the ground of his own reconciliation with life.

Let us briefly survey the plot of the story. Prospero, Duke of Milan, and his three-year-old daughter, Miranda, are put to sea in a rotten boat by his usurping brother Antonio with the connivance of Alonzo, King of Naples. The scene opens twelve years after the crime, with Prospero and Miranda on an enchanted island. Prospero through his great knowledge is master of the spirits, both good and evil, and controls all the energies of nature. The King of Naples and the usurping duke, with the Prince Ferdinand, are on the sea, returning from the wedding of the king's daughter. Through Ariel, the Enchanter raises a frightful storm on the deep. The company is washed into the sea, and the prince separated from his father, each thinking the other lost. Prospero, as overruling Providence, punished the King of Naples for his sin by remorse, even as God had punished Richard III: —

> "O, it is monstrous! monstrous!
> Methought the billows spoke and told me of it;
> The winds did sing it to me; and the thunder,
> That deep and dreadful organ pipe, pronounced
> The name of Prosper." [1]

Antonio, Sebastian, and Caliban are given opportunity to reveal their evil natures, but are foiled from frustrating the designs of Prospero, — for man deviseth in his heart, but God directs

[1] Act III, sc. iii.

his steps. When Prospero's enemies are all "knit up in their distractions," and are in the gloom where tragedy lets fall the final curtain, the real nature of the power which inflicts the seeming evil is made known. There has been sin and retribution, there is also reconciliation. Prospero exclaims: —

> "Though with their high wrongs I am strook to the quick,
> Yet, with my nobler reason 'gainst my fury
> Do I take part. The rarer action is
> In virtue than in vengeance; they being penitent,
> The sole drift of my purpose doth extend
> Not a frown farther." [1]

When his clemency is revealed Alonzo, the king, is melted to repentance and confession. He also restores the dukedom. Antonio is forgiven, but there is no genuine reconciliation between the two brothers, for there is no contrition on the part of the usurper. Even Caliban learns his lesson.

> "I'll be wise hereafter,
> And seek for grace."

The whole drift of the plot is an expansion of the fine statement of Henry V: "There is some soul of goodness in things evil." This "soul of goodness" rules even at the centre of the universe, evil is so constrained as to issue in final good, men are guided by a supreme Good Will which punishes, but also works benignantly for reconciliation. Surrounded by the mystery, inexplicable because of our partial vision, —

[1] Act V, sc. i.

> "Do not infest your mind by beating on
> The strangeness of this business." [1]

In time we shall know the whole, —

> "Till then, be cheerful,
> And think of each thing well." [2]

In the characters of Hermione and Prospero we have a deeper note than is struck in the tragedies. Sin is permitted to do its worst, but it has met a supreme power. The "soul of goodness," in humanity and in the universe, patiently endures all that evil can do, and by steady and effluent good will disarms evil, and brings it to repentance and final reconciliation.

Once again the master hand touches this great theme of reconciliation with life. In 1613 Shakespeare with Fletcher perfected Henry VIII for the stage. The interest centres in the calamities falling upon Katharine and Wolsey. The queen is a disinterested, high-souled woman, and even Wolsey, despite his chicaneries, is at heart a true man. Here again the blind wrath of man dashes against goodness, but there is no tragedy. The queen, deprived of her station, displays a moral grandeur which shames the malignity of her enemies. The reader feels that the real victory is with her. She has triumphed over evil, and wrong has unwittingly worked righteousness. And even Wolsey, though he has ventured too wantonly on the sea of glory, can be reconciled

---

[1] Act V, sc. ii.   [2] Act V, sc. i.

to his fate. His troubles have exalted him above their power to hurt.

> "Never so truly happy, my good Cromwell.
> I know myself now; and I feel within me
> A peace above all earthly dignities,
> A still and quiet conscience."[1]

In considering the light which the genius of Shakespeare has thrown upon our subject, we find that he emphasizes as persistently and as unmistakably as Æschylus, Sophocles, or Dante the supremacy of a moral order and its sure recoil when the equilibrium is disturbed. With Dante he recognizes the necessity of repentance and confession and the impulse of a contrite soul to expiate, so far as possible, the wrong done. With Dante he also affirms the supremacy of goodness over evil. Goodness meets evil, suffers its rage, bears patiently with it, and wins it to repentance. This triumph of goodness in our own lives reconciles us to the severe process by which it was achieved, while our trust that the dark forces of nature and society are controlled by an Infinite mercy, and eventuate in a good end, is the ground of our reconcilement with life.

We ask the reader's especial attention to the consideration which follows. In the closing scene of "The Tempest" Prospero says to Alonzo:—

> "Let us not burden our rememberance with
> A heaviness that's gone."[2]

---

[1] Act III, sc. ii.   [2] Act V, sc. i.

The past may well be forgotten in the joy of the final issue. But if the result had been otherwise, and any disaster had ensued, then an untormented memory would have been impossible. Prospero, Alonzo, Wolsey, Katharine, all can look back with unembittered recollection upon a shadowed and stormy past, because of its felicitous termination. Their eyes were opened to the soul of goodness in things evil, goodness had triumphed over evil and subdued it, making it subserve righteous ends. Prospero can enter into unrestrained friendship with his former enemies because his good will has prevailed and turned tragedy into success. If the tragic forces had won, if Miranda had been dishonored by Caliban, and Antonio had ruled insolently in Milan, while Prospero was foiled and defeated, then the Enchanter would not have been reconciled without doing violence to his better nature. He could *forgive* freely and righteously, if his foes recognized the true nature of their crimes, were genuinely contrite, and brought forth fruit meet for repentance. But the more difficult task of reconciliation is accomplished only when goodness has wrought its perfect work. This triumph of goodness makes possible Prospero's acquiescence in his past, gives peace to his memory, and reconciles him to the severe trials of his life. In his vision of the transcendency of the divine Power, the supreme Wisdom, and the primal

Love, Dante found peace for his tempestuous spirit. In the supernatural honors paid to Œdipus, Sophocles hints that the joy of the consummation would remove all heaviness from the burdened mind of his hero. The atonement for the memory, the Lethe in which the past is forgotten, is the apprehension by faith of that victorious goodness which works through faults, mistakes, sins, to a glorious result. This alone makes possible a reconciliation with one's past.

VIII

MILTON

When I consider how my light is spent
   Ere half my days, in this dark world and wide,
   And that one talent which is death to hide,
   Lodg'd with me useless, though my soul more bent
To serve therewith my Maker, and present
   My true account, lest he returning chide;
   "Doth God exact day labour, light denied?"
   I fondly ask: but Patience, to prevent
That murmur, soon replies, "God doth not need
   Either man's work, or his own gifts; who best
   Bear his mild yoke, they serve him best: his state
Is kingly; thousands at his bidding speed,
   And post o'er land and ocean without rest
   They also serve who only stand and wait."

                                  JOHN MILTON.

CHAPTER VIII

MILTON

MILTON's "great organ note of song" grows deep and majestic as it pours forth the story —

> "Of man's first disobedience, and the fruit
> Of that forbidden tree, whose mortal taste
> Brought death into the world and all our woe,
> With loss of Eden, till one greater Man
> Restore us and regain the blissful seat."

His theme in "Paradise Lost" and "Paradise Regained" is the one with which we have grown so familiar, — Sin, Retribution, Reconciliation. His treatment of sin is very different from that of either Dante or Shakespeare. Dante portrays iniquity in its final estate, a hideous, disgusting, loathsome thing whose fit symbol is the monstrous, bloody, half-dead brute, Lucifer. Shakespeare represents sin as it is to-day in bad men, cunning, malignant, reptilian, finding in Iago its fit expression. Milton, however, shows us sin at its beginning, when it is fascinating with a lustre and glory which it does not have in the end. His Satan is of necessity a nobler person than Dante's Lucifer. Yet Milton gives prophetic glimpses of what the ultimate issue will be. In the beginning of "Paradise Lost" Satan appears as a majestic being, titanic in force, possessing still some of his original splendor, like the sun seen through the misty air. He is an archangel ruined, and, full of primal energy, is capable of putting to proof the high supremacy of heaven's perpetual King. Suddenly out of the infernal deep Pandemonium arises; seated on his throne of royal state Satan unfolds to his peers in words of lofty eloquence his vast plans of rebellion. Passing beyond the gates of Sin and Death, he works his grievous way through chaos till he comes in sight of Eden. Here he falls into many doubts, but, unwilling to submit to the will of God, he confirms himself in evil. As craft and serpentine deceit take the place of open war, the deeper sin brings the deeper ruin to his nature. Returning to his followers, he ascends the throne from which but a short time before he had spoken such heroic words. Refulgent with permissive glory he begins to recount his exploits; but, pausing to receive the expected applause of the Stygian throng, he is amazed to hear —

> "from innumerable tongues,
> A dismal universal hiss."[1]

Not long did he wonder; his face began to draw sharp and spare, his arms clung to his ribs, his legs entwined each other, and his noble eloquence changed into a hiss!

[1] *Paradise Lost*, x, 507.

> "Down he fell
> A monstrous serpent on his belly prone,
> Reluctant, but in vain : a greater power
> Now rul'd him, punish'd in the shape he sinn'd,
> According to his doom ; he would have spoke,
> But hiss to hiss returned with forked tongue
> To forked tongue, for now were all transformed
> Alike to serpents all." [1]

Sin begins in pride, grows cunning, treacherous, serpentine, and ultimates in a perverted mind which cannot distinguish reality from illusion, and what seems fair fruit turns to bitter ashes in the mouth. After the hellish crew had been turned to serpents, there sprang up a grove hard by,—

> "laden with fair fruit, like that
> Which grew in paradise, the bait of Eve
> Us'd by the tempter : on that prospect strange
> Their earnest eyes they fix'd, imagining
> For one forbidden tree a multitude
> Now risen, to work them further woe or shame :
> Yet parch'd with scalding thirst and hunger fierce,
> Though to delude them sent, could not abstain,
> But on they roll'd in heaps, and up the trees
> Climbing sat thicker than the snaky locks
> That curl'd Megæra : greedily they pluck'd
> The fruitage fair to sight, like that which grew
> Near that bituminous lake where Sodom flam'd,
> This more delusive not the touch, but taste
> Deceiv'd ; they fondly thinking to allay
> Their appetite with gust, instead of fruit
> Chew'd bitter ashes, which the offended taste
> With spattering noise rejected : oft they assay'd
> Hunger and thirst constraining ; drugg'd as oft,
> With hatefullest disrelish writh'd their jaws
> With soot and cinders fill'd ; so oft they fell
> Into the same illusion." [2]

[1] *Paradise Lost*, x, 513–520. [2] *Ibid.*, 550–571.

The character of sin which most impressed Dante was its insensibility. The sinful mind was dead to the presence of God in his universe. It failed to discern the gleam of the divine presence in the providences of life. Milton, on the other hand, emphasized most of all the lawlessness of evil, the wild anarchy which it introduced into the world, its tempests of passion, its audacious rebellion against heaven's eternal King.

In his treatment of reconciliation the Puritan poet gives great prominence to a principle strangely neglected by theology, but to which our aroused social consciousness compels us to accord due consideration. Sin's most dreadful curse is not its effect upon the one committing it, but the havoc wrought in the lives and hopes of others. To a contrite soul the woe which his sin flings upon the innocent is of more moment than the effect upon himself. A gospel would be an offense which shows him how to escape from the turbid stream of iniquity, but gives no word of hope for the victims of his wrong who are still struggling in the murky current. The consequences as well as the causes of sin must be included in any adequate salvation. A social as well as an individual redemption is needed. Otherwise the sorrow entailed upon others would be forever a haunting spectre. No redeemed soul could live in eternal light with such a shadowed memory. There must be a reconciliation with one's past, a tranquillity in the presence of sin's awful results, ere eternal peace can settle upon the soul. How this joyous serenity in the face of the fell entailment of sin may be obtained through Christ's work of redemption Milton shows with singular clearness and impressive emphasis.

After Adam had sinned, he would have deserved contempt if his supreme thought had been to escape the penalties of his transgression. Most truly does Milton declare that the bitterest woe of the first transgressor was the contemplation of the dreadful consequences visited upon his descendants. The thought of this awful entailment overcomes him, and he falls upon the ground in frenzied agony. His imperious need is an atonement which will provide for his sin's death-dealing effects upon others; it is such a view of his past as will enable him to forgive himself. A revelation of God's love and pardon to him as an individual would be utterly inadequate. It is a social and not a personal atonement he craves.

Milton here confronts the same problem which absorbed the attention of Æschylus. What power is sufficient to meet and stay the curse of sin when it is once unleashed? The Greek tragedian viewed the question microscopically as it related to the family, while Milton surveys it in the larger aspect of humanity; yet their replies are essentially the same. The curse of the house of Atreus is stayed when it lights upon Orestes, a good man who represents both contending parties and is obedient to the divine oracles. And Milton declares that the head of the serpent is bruised unto death by the heel of one who as Son of Man and of God by his perfect obedience wins the victory.

When Adam sees his disobedience in the light of its destructive effects on his descendants, he repents. His remorse is not chiefly for his personal loss, but for the far-reaching misery which will enfold others. That which will be to him a gospel is not the offer of a Heavenly Paradise, if he obediently endures his earthly wanderings; but a revelation of how the dire consequences of his transgression are either expunged or turned to good. Without such knowledge of good triumphing over his evil there can be no soul rest for him, either in this world or the world to come. It is precisely this assuaging of the pain of memory through a vision of victorious righteousness for which Milton provides. Michael is sent to the sin-cursed Adam for his comfort. The angel takes him to a high hill —

> "from whose top
> The hemisphere of earth in clearest ken
> Stretch'd out to the amplest reach of prospect lay." [1]

From his eyes the film was removed by three drops from the well of life instilled, and he beholds in astounding vision the unfolding grace of God in redemption, until —

[1] *Paradise Lost,* xi, 378.

> "he, who comes thy Saviour, shall recure
> Not by destroying Satan, but his works
> In thee and in thy seed." [1]

Raptured by the vision of Christ's perfect victory over sin —

> "our sire
> Replete with joy and wonder thus reply'd.
> O goodness infinite, goodness immense!
> That all this good of evil shall produce,
> And evil turn to good; more wonderful
> Than that by which creation first brought forth
> Light out of darkness! full of doubt I stand,
> Whether I shall repent me now of sin
> By me done and occasion'd, or rejoice
> Much more, that much more good thereof shall spring.
> To God more glory, more good will to men
> From God, and over wrath grace shall abound." [2]

When the vision had passed our first parent descended "greatly in peace of thought." He had found what he most craved, — a Lethe for his memory, a reconciliation with his past, a social and cosmic atonement, won by Christ's high triumph over sin.

Before the "Paradise Lost" was published, young Ellwood, a friend of Milton, borrowed the manuscript. On returning it he said to the poet: "Thou hast said much here of Paradise lost, but what hast thou to say of Paradise found?" The poet sat for some time in a state of abstraction, but returned no answer. "Paradise Regained" was his final reply. The result is radically different from what the prevalent theology of the time,

---

[1] *Paradise Lost*, xii, 393.   [2] *Ibid.*, xii, 467-478.

with its strong accent on the sufferings of Christ, would have led us to suppose. We should have expected Milton to find his theme in the cup dripping with darkness and agony which the Father held to the lips of Christ in Gethsemane and in the fierce pains and spiritual gloom of Calvary; for had not theology taught for a thousand years that the sufferings of Christ satisfied the righteous judgments of God?

The insight of the poet pierces further into truth than the logic of the schoolman. Paradise is regained by the victory, not the pains, of Christ.

> " Winning by conquest what the first man lost
> By fallacy unpriz'd." [1]

So the temptation in the wilderness was chosen, that triumph and not suffering might be the dominant note.

> "There shall he first lay down the rudiments
> Of his great warfare, ere I send him forth
> To conquer sin and death, the two grand foes,
> By humiliation and strong sufferance.
> His weakness shall o'ercome satanic strength,
> And all the world, and mass of sinful flesh;
> That all the angels and æthereal powers,
> They now, and men hereafter, may discern,
> From what consummate virtue I have chose
> This perfect man, by merit call'd my Son,
> To earn salvation for the sons of men." [2]

The schools have taught expiation by suffering, a divine wrath appeased by torture, the pain of

---

[1] *Paradise Lost*, i, 154.   [2] *Ibid.*, i, 157–167.

one accepted by a legal fiction for the condemnation of many. Milton opens a sunnier, healthier region of thought. To make forgiveness rational, there must indeed be a satisfaction given both to justice and to love; but it is no legal fiction that is offered, — a real amendment is made; the hurt of sin is healed; its direful consequences are changed to good.

Milton has here given us an element in reconciliation which is of commanding importance. There must be a social and cosmic atonement, an actual repair of the havoc of sin, else the individual whose sins have polluted the stream of humanity and entailed suffering upon others can never have an untormenting conscience or a tranquil memory. His Lethe is the insight of faith into the nature of God and the complete divine victory over all evil.

IX

GEORGE ELIOT

Sin and its reaction, pain eating away the sin, purity and wisdom through the suffering of sin, sin and its disclosure through conscience, — what else do we find in the great masterpieces of fiction and poetry, not indeed with slavish uniformity, but as a dominant thought? Hawthorne wrote of little else; it gives eternal freshness to his pages. It runs like a golden thread through the works of George Eliot and makes them other than they seem. For the most part the literature of the Occident is Christian; I mean the great literature; but we must not expect to find all of Christianity in any one author. Working, spirit-like, its method has been that of searching out those gifted ones whose mental note responded to some note in itself, and set them singing or speaking in that key. Thus it has worked, and we must look for Christianity in Literature not as though listening to one singer after another, but rather to a whole choir. — T. T. MUNGER.

CHAPTER IX

GEORGE ELIOT

To avoid having our investigation extended to such a length as to become wearisome, and to prevent needless reiteration, in the study of modern authors, of principles with which we are now familiar, we shall confine our attention to those books which treat of some special phase of reconciliation. This method may elicit the criticism that the authors hereinafter studied are given inadequate consideration, yet our theme will thereby gain much in clearness; and we hope that the investigation will commend itself as trustworthy, even though confined to so narrow limits.

In "Adam Bede" the problem of reconciliation with one's past is treated in a very different mood from that pervading "Paradise Lost." It is necessary to recall the story only in barest outline. The *dramatis personae* who are of interest to us for our present purpose are Arthur Donnithorne, well-meaning, impulsive, heir to the estate of Hayslope; Adam Bede, a strong, clear-headed, noble-minded carpenter; and Hetty Sorrel, pretty, vain, and shallow. Arthur's feeling for Hetty was a passing fancy, hot and passionate, working her ruin. Adam Bede loved her from the deeps of his manly nature, and purposed making her his wife. Vividly and with rare power has George Eliot portrayed poor Hetty's sufferings, the birth of her child, her wanderings, her frenzied attempt to abandon the little one, and her sentence to death for child murder. When Arthur learned the awful results of what he had considered but a temporary lapse from virtue, with whole-hearted repentance and with tireless energy he set himself to do what he could to repair the evil, and succeeded in having Hetty's death sentence changed to one of transportation. The next day at evening the two men met by accident. Their warm friendship had been annulled by an irretrievable wrong. What reconciliation is possible! Adam's indignation was just and righteous. He certainly could not easily forgive one who had deeply injured him and ruined his promised bride. But when he sees the marks of suffering in Arthur's face, and learns of his determination to leave Hayslope and exile himself rather than have Adam and his friends forsake the estate, the heart of the sturdy carpenter is touched, and he gives his hand in forgiveness. His just indignation has been propitiated by Arthur's contrition, his suffering, and his endeavors to undo as much of the wrong as he can. Without such propitiation forgiveness would have been impossible. And Arthur's desire was surely not simply for happiness and personal release from the awkward position in which his sin had placed him. His supreme purpose was to lessen the evil consequences of an irrevocable past. Yet the thought which shadowed them both was well expressed by Adam: "There's a sort o' damage, sir, that can't be made up for." The irrevocableness of the past is one of George Eliot's fundamental teachings. A sin once launched into the world leaves a trail of blood and tears which can neither be forgotten nor effaced. A breach once made cannot be repaired. The reconciliation of Arthur Donnithorne and Adam Bede is only a friendly union hallowed by a common sorrow. It is a shadowed, incomplete reconciliation. The atonement is imperfect, for the consequences of evil cannot be stayed or their havoc amended. Poor Hetty was flung body and soul into an unlighted abyss of woe, and the memory of the tragedy casts a black and dismal shadow on the minds of her two lovers. Such measure of reconciliation as is possible, according to the rarely gifted and comprehensive mind of our author, is won by repentance, confession, and a suffering energy repairing in some degree the evil done. Arthur's suffering, his genuine repentance, and his partial rectification of the wrong propitiate a just indignation. Beyond this the author does not go. Arthur's last words were: "But you told me the truth when you said to me once, 'There's a sort of wrong that can never be made up for.'" George Eliot does not —

> "forecast the years,
> And find in loss a gain to match,
> Or reach a hand through time to catch
> The far-off interest of tears."

She does not see with Milton a "Goodness immense" throwing its healing light and power into the abyss of the loss, nor does she say with Tennyson : —

> "O, yet we trust that somehow good
> Will be the final goal of ill,
> . . . . . .
> That not one life shall be destroy'd,
> Or cast as rubbish to the void,
> When God hath made the pile complete."

X

HAWTHORNE

We meet at every turn, with Hawthorne, his favorite fancy of communicated sorrows and inevitable atonements. Life is an experience in which we expiate the sins of others in the intervals of expiating our own. — HENRY JAMES.

What renders the "Scarlet Letter" one of the greatest of books is the sleuth-hound thoroughness with which sin is traced up and down and into every corner of the heart and life, and even into nature, where it transforms all things. Shakespeare paints with a larger brush, and sets it in great tragic happenings; but its windings, the subtle infusion of itself into every faculty and impressing itself upon outward things, are left for Hawthorne's unapproachable skill. — T. T. MUNGER.

CHAPTER X

HAWTHORNE

THE most powerful work of fiction which this country has produced is undoubtedly "The Scarlet Letter." As one moves with absorbed interest from page to page of this fascinating book, its resemblance to Dante's "Purgatorio" becomes impressive. Hester Prynne must change the scarlet letter A from a badge of infamy to a symbol of purity. Dante must wipe the seven P's from his forehead. The method of cleansing the stain of sin from the soul is identical. Dante sums it up in these words: *confessio, contritio, satisfactio*, symbolized in the three steps leading to the gate of justification. Over them all Hester climbed with patient feet, while Dimmesdale would tread them all but the clear mirror of confession. In many instances the language of the two books has a pronounced similarity. Not that Hawthorne consciously copied from Dante, for there is reason to believe that his familiarity with Italian literature began after "The Scarlet Letter" was written. But the sombre genius of the New Englander, as it penetrated into the spiritual problem which the Florentine had mined, found the same golden veins of truth. The scene of one is in Boston, and of the other on the Holy Mountain; but in both the interest centres in tracing the rugged and fiery path by which liberty from the stain and power of sin is attained. The weird and gloomy genius of the Protestant has drawn an even more terrible picture than did that of the mediæval Catholic. Hawthorne's purpose was to show how Hester Prynne, who for the sin of adultery was condemned to wear the scarlet letter A exposed upon her bosom, and Arthur Dimmesdale, her unrevealed partner in guilt, purified their souls through purgatorial sufferings. So closely do the minds of these two powerful writers keep together in unfolding their common thought that sometimes almost identical forms of expression and experience are used. In one place Hawthorne employs a sentence to describe the lot of his hero that reminds us very forcibly of Dante's famous account of his own experiences. Mr. Dimmesdale had chosen single blessedness; therefore he is compelled " to eat his unsavory morsel always at another's board, and endure the lifelong chill which must be his lot who seeks to warm himself only at another's fireside." [1] Very similar is Dante's statement of his own homeless condition, in the well-known prophecy of Cacciaguida: —

[1] *The Scarlet Letter*, chap. ix.

"Thou shalt have proof how savoureth of salt
The bread of others, and how hard a road
The going up and down another's stairs." [1]

No writer of recent times has given such conspicuous emphasis to the need of confession as Hawthorne. Arthur Dimmesdale was sincerely repentant, and eager to expiate his sin; but his quivering, supersensitive nature shrank from honest confession. But without confession his tortured soul is divided against itself. He must be known exactly as he is.

"Happy are you, Hester, that wear the scarlet letter openly upon your bosom! Mine burns in secret! Thou little knowest what a relief it is, after the torment of a seven years' cheat, to look into an eye that recognizes me for what I am! Had I a friend — or were it my worst enemy! — to whom, when sickened with the praises of all other men, I could daily betake myself and be known as the vilest of all sinners, methinks my soul might keep itself alive thereby. Even this much of truth would save me. But now it is all falsehood! — all emptiness! — all death!" [2]

Yet a disclosure of himself to an individual is not sufficient. His sin had been against the community. He is a member of the community, and to that he must be reconciled. Therefore he is made to stand upon the scaffold with Hester, that he may be seen by the world in his true character.

[1] *Par.* xvii, 58–60.   [2] *The Scarlet Letter*, chap. xvii.

As he approached the place, old Roger Chillingworth exclaimed: " Hadst thou sought the whole earth over there was no one place so secret — no high place nor lowly place, where thou couldst have escaped me, — save on this very scaffold!"[1] Only by confession can he escape the power of his implacable enemy. When at last, amid the great awe of the multitude, he ascends the steps and reveals the red stigma on his own bosom, symbol of his terrible secret, he dies in triumphant peace. This psychological need of confession Hawthorne again emphasizes in " The Marble Faun." The spotless soul of Hilda could not enfold the guilty secret of the murder she had witnessed. The memory would not cease its torments until she found peace in unburdening her spirit — Protestant though she was — in a confessional.

Another element in reconciliation is distinctly seen in the gloom and light of " The Scarlet Letter." When Hester, in the earlier chapters, was on the scaffold, she was nerved to encounter the taunts and merriment of the multitude; but when instead of jeers she confronted a silence, solemn, judicial, awed, it was to her wild nature oppressive beyond endurance. Severe as the Puritans undoubtedly were, the indignation the community felt at a destructive social evil was just. With this righteous condemnation of her fault Hester must deal, if reconciliation is to follow retribution.

[1] *Ibid.*, chap. xxiii.

Repentance and confession are not sufficient; there must be an appeasement of a just hostility to an influence which has worked and may still work injury to the community. Amends must be made, the effects of evil must be overcome; Hester must bring forth fruits meet for repentance; but what gives that fruit its value is that her new character and good deeds counteract the contagious evil of her former life and make her a help and not a menace to the community.

Through long years of service she propitiates — let us not shrink from the word, it represents a reality — the outraged moral sense of the town by the pure womanliness of her character and the beneficence of her deeds. Had she retired from the scaffold merely penitent, but with no settled purpose to atone for the wrong, her neighbors could not have given her an unreserved confidence. Had she lived a life of ease and prosperity, the just condemnation of the community would not have been allayed. She must suffer, else sin will seem a slight thing, easily wiped out. Her sufferings must be great enough to make the crime appear hideous, and purity attractive. Without the shedding of blood, there is no remission. The offending person must live a sacrificial life if society is to forgive.

This is another aspect of Hawthorne's fundamental principle of confession. Not only must the individual know and confess his sin, but the sin must be so displayed and condemned that it shall appear loathsome to all. It is not to be glossed over or ignored, but known in its enormity by the forgiven and the forgiver, if reconciliation is to be rational and complete. Thus does Hester propitiate the righteous recoil of her social world from her by a suffering, benevolent life which robs her sin of all its fascination, transforms her character into a source of light and not darkness, and sets in motion numberless currents of good which compensate for the evil she had done.

Hester had committed a sin which militated against the social well-being. Society is righteous in the condemnation of the sin, and cannot fully forgive her until she is no longer in any way representative of it. Repentance and confession but partially release her. She is still associated with it. Its nature will be judged by its painful effects upon her. If she lives a life of luxurious ease, her sin will appear but a soft infirmity, and not the destructive thing it is. Only by an earnest self-forgetfulness can the taint of sin be purged and she become to the community a savor of life and not of death. Without such evident contrition and conquest of her sin there can be no thorough propitiation of a proper social judgment, and without such propitiation Hester cannot enter harmoniously into the present life of the community.

It should be noted that Hester won a greater degree of reconciliation with her neighbors than it was possible for Arthur Donnithorne to gain from Adam Bede. Adam genuinely forgave Arthur, but could not be perfectly reconciled to him, for the shadow of an irremediable loss prevented. Hester, however, was able by her life of faithfulness and good deeds so far to overcome the evil effects of her transgression upon both herself and the town in which her lot was cast that she was not only forgiven, but received in abundant measure evidences of her neighbors' reconciliation with her. Both Arthur Donnithorne and Hester were forgiven, but to Hester was granted a greater degree of approval from the community she injured, because the social influences of her sin were checked and conquered by her chastened and benignant life, while Adam Bede could not have the same feelings of complacency, as his loss was irreparable. Reconciliation must be won by the complete triumph of good over evil.

XI

HOSEA AND TENNYSON

Of all the prophets he [Hosea] was the first to break into the full aspect of the Divine Mercy — to learn and to proclaim that God is love. But he was worthy to do so by the patient love of his own heart toward another who for years had outraged all his trust and tenderness. As he had loved Gomer, so God had loved Israel, past hope, against hate, through ages of ingratitude and apostasy. Quivering with his own pain, Hosea had exhausted all human care and affection for figures to express the Divine tenderness, and he declares God's love to be deeper than all the passion of men, and broader than all their patience : *How can I give thee up, Ephraim ? How can I let thee go, Israel ? I will not execute the fierceness of Mine anger.* — GEORGE ADAM SMITH.

> And all is well, tho' faith and form
> Be sunder'd in the night of fear ;
> Well roars the storm to those that hear
> A deeper voice across the storm.
>
> TENNYSON.

CHAPTER XI

HOSEA AND TENNYSON

HERETOFORE Occidental literature, Greek, Italian, English, has occupied our attention. It will increase the range and effectiveness of our conclusions to glance into Oriental life. We open the Bible not to quote proof texts, but to ascertain how reconciliation was actually worked out by living souls in earlier days and in another civilization. As the need of propitiation has been brought to our attention both by Hawthorne and George Eliot, we shall first study the experiences of Hosea, in whose griefs the same necessity finds exposition. Behind the somewhat cryptic sentences in which the prophet tells his sorrow, the story constructs itself in this fashion.

Hosea, a young Hebrew, refined, pure-minded, high-souled, marries Gomer, whom he believes to be as chaste as himself. How soon the shadow of suspicion of her unfaithfulness fell upon him we do not know, but her first child he acknowledged as his own. When the second child, a girl, was born, he called her " Unloved," or " That-never-knew-a-father's-pity." The third infant he named " Not-my-people." For a long time he bore with his impure companion, but at length she drifted from his home to go with strange paramours. She fell lower and lower, until, like members of her class, she ended in slavery. Yet all this time the eager heart of the prophet yearned for her, and his love followed her from step to step in her downward course, for the strength of love depends not upon the worthiness of the object loved, but upon the greatness of the heart which loves. Finally, when she had reached the depths of wretchedness, he bought her back at the price of a slave.

> "Weeping blinding tears
> I took her to myself and paid the price
> (Strange contrast to the dowry of her youth
> When first I wooed her) : and she came again
> To dwell beneath my roof."

Yet he could not restore her immediately to the old relationship. "And I said to her, For many days shalt thou abide for me alone: thou shalt not play the harlot, thou shalt not be for any husband; and I for my part also shall be so towards thee." Although the prophet's love had not faltered in his purpose to rescue his wife, yet his pure soul recoiled in the presence of her defilement. She was still too thoroughly identified with her sin, too stained by it, to admit of perfect reconciliation. Hosea felt that there must be an expiatory suffering, which should both purify her and propitiate an instinctive and just reserve on his part.

> "In silence and alone,
> In shame and sorrow, wailing, fast and prayer
> She must blot out the stain that made her life
> One long pollution."

In the fires of his experiences Hosea forged his evangel. If his love was so leal that it followed Gomer in all her wanderings until she was won back to righteousness, surely Jehovah, having loved Israel, would love them unto the end, and would redeem them in righteousness.

The principles upon which reconciliation is made possible are clear. The efficient cause comes not from the transgressor, but from the great heart sinned against. Love suffering and exhaustless sought out the defiled one. Yet all exhibitions of Hosea's affection did not win Gomer to the paths of rectitude. She came to herself in view of the consequences of her sin rather than through the persuasions of the prophet's love. Still it was the unwearying love of Hosea that found her at the psychical moment, pardoned, and brought her back. But holy love cannot ignore moral distinctions. There is an impassable barrier between purity and impurity. The wrongdoer must not only repent, but must also live in such a manner as to realize and honor fundamental moral distinctions, thus appeasing an aversion which is both instinctive and righteous. Sin taints and stains; even genuine repentance does not at once purify and render the evil an alien thing, so entirely disassociated from the sinful one that it offers no obstacle to complacent love. It is too definitely associated with the perpetrator to be treated as though it were not. Marvelous as was Hosea's affection, both in its strength and in its tirelessness, it was too pure and sensitive not to shrink from his polluted wife. Something must be done, or felt, or thought before a benevolent love can become complacent. Hosea would propitiate this instinctive aversion of his own refined nature, the moral sense of the community, and Gomer's natural disgust with herself, by enjoining upon her to live such a life of purity that she should become a new creature dissociated from her past, and able to be received without detriment into the old relationship.

Tennyson, in the "Idylls of the King," recounts precisely the same experiences and feelings. King Arthur began his reign with a noble ideal of a just and prosperous kingdom. His knights of the Round Table furthered his fair design until the hapless day when the queen fell a victim to her guilty love for Lancelot. "Red ruin and the breaking up of laws" was the result. Arthur's exalted ideal was shattered, his kingdom rent with civil war, and overrun by an invasion of barbarian hordes. The queen fled to a convent, where Arthur sought her out ere he went to engage in that last fateful battle of the West. As

Guinevere heard the clang of his mailed feet along the cloister halls, she fell prone upon the floor in deep repentance. The king is Tennyson's ideal of noblest man, and he came not in anger.

> "Lo! I forgive thee, as Eternal God
> Forgives; do thou for thine own soul the rest.
> . . . .
> I cannot touch thy lips, they are not mine.
> . . . .
> I cannot take thy hand; that too is flesh
> And in the flesh thou hast sinn'd; and mine own flesh
> Here looking down on thine polluted, cries
> 'I loathe thee;' yet not less, O Guinevere,
> For I was ever virgin save for thee,
> My love through flesh hath wrought into my life
> So far, that my doom is, I love thee still.
> Perchance, and thou so purify thy soul,
> And so thou lean on our fair father Christ,
> Hereafter in that world where all are pure
> We two may meet before high God, and thou
> Wilt spring to me, and claim me thine, and know
> I am thine husband — not a smaller soul,
> Nor Lancelot, nor another. Leave me that,
> I charge thee, my last hope."

The king loved and forgave the unhappy queen, and yet he could not take her to his breast in one last embrace, before he went to his death. An instinctive revulsion from her polluted body restrained him. There could not be perfect reconciliation until through Christ her very nature was changed.

The queen, too, recognized this stain.

> "The shadow of another cleaves to me,
> And makes me one pollution."

Yet reconciliation is not impossible: —

> "In mine own heart I can live down sin,
> And be his mate hereafter in the heavens
> Before high God."

And so in "almsdeed and in prayer" she wears out —

> "The sombre close of that voluptuous day
> Which wrought the ruin of my lord, the king."

Hosea and Tennyson both alike attest that the holiest love conceivable in a human bosom is checked in its passion for perfect reconciliation by a revulsion from evil which cannot be ignored, but must be allayed.

XII

JOB, THE SUFFERING SERVANT, PSALM XVII, SYMONDS, WHITMAN, WHITTIER

And I saw that there was an Ocean of Darkness and Death; but an Infinite Ocean of Light and Love flowed over the Ocean of Darkness; and in that I saw the Infinite Love of God. — GEORGE FOX.

> My hope is that a sun will pierce
> The thickest cloud earth ever stretched;
> That after Last returns the First,
> Though a wide compass round be fetched;
> That what began best, can't end worst,
> Nor what God blessed once, prove accurst.
> ROBERT BROWNING.

CHAPTER XII

JOB, THE SUFFERING SERVANT, PSALM XVII, SYMONDS, WHITMAN, WHITTIER

THERE is another phase of our subject well worthy of consideration — a phase touched upon by Dante and more fully developed by Shakespeare. Most of the plots we have studied trace the methods by which persons alienated by sin have been joined in a harmonious union. Life in its darkest aspects has engaged our attention. We have contemplated exceptional experiences. In the ordinary course of existence we do not often confront such tragedy and its widespreading gloom. Humanity's most familiar problem is to become reconciled to the limitations and discipline of life itself. The world is not to our mind. The conditions upon which life is given to us are not as we would have them. We dream our dreams, project our glowing ideals, lay our plans for the future, only to be thwarted by circumstances beyond our control. We choose our path and walk in it with joy until we find ourselves confronted by some stern obstacle of duty rising sheer before us, and we turn back with rebellious hearts. To make " I will " surrender joyfully to " I must" requires many a severe battle. " Must " is probably the most disliked word in our language. The lover never speaks it. The devotee of liberty will die rather than obey it. Yet to bring the individual will into joyful acquiescence with inexorable necessity is life's hardest task and most important achievement. Conscious sin is not in ordinary experience the chief deterrent to union with God. Rather the difficulty lies in adjusting our lives to the inevitable order of events. Religion, in the opinion of Professor James, is an "enthusiastic temper of espousal toward the universe." It is the glad acceptance of God's ways with men. It is loving him with the mind. Thus it is reconciliation with God's providential revelation of himself in individual and national history, rather than the forgiveness of sins, which most interests the modern man.

It is in the book of Job that this problem finds its classical and noblest expression.

In the early days the simple faith of the Hebrew was satisfied with the belief that suffering was Jehovah's penalty upon wrong-doing, and happiness and prosperity his reward of righteousness. But a broader view of life and a clear knowledge of how often the innocent are afflicted while the wicked flourish, easily disproved the primitive, undiscriminating philosophy.

The book of Job grew out of that period of intense spiritual struggle when the Hebrew mind

— always keenly alive to the eternal mysteries — grappled afresh with masculine energy the still unsolved enigma of the meaning of the evil which settles upon the righteous. The three friends bring their little systems of theology — the accepted notions of the day — to comfort the deep, tumultuous, sorrowing heart of Job. A few months before the patriarch would have agreed with their philosophies, but his bitter experiences had opened new abysses of life, his soul had gone down into a darkness too profound to be reached by the sickly light of their childish theories. Fiercely he retorts, silencing their chatter and boldly asserting his integrity. When his lacerated heart has exhausted itself in useless ragings, and his mind has come to realize its own impotency in the presence of the infinite mystery, then God answers Job out of the whirlwind, teaching his stricken spirit that not in speculations about God, but in the consciousness of God himself, is the final peace and the unravelment of all difficulties.

The significant religious teaching of this brilliant book is that suffering is not merely God's punishment of wrong-doing; it is also one of his methods of testing character; it is something to be heroically endured that it may accomplish its perfect work, and the recompense is that vision of divine grace which only can give peace. The sufferer is satisfied that God in all this disciplinary training has been just. The reward atones for all the pain, and he can say joyfully: —

> "I had heard of thee by the hearing of the ear;
> But now mine eye seeth thee."

In the power of that vision all querulous complaints seem to be a rebellion against divine love, and the penitent exclaims: —

> "Wherefore I abhor myself, and repent
> In dust and ashes."[1]

It is this revelation of God to the soul and the soul's answering trust in the justice and mercy of God's providential dealings that is the full and adequate compensation. The afflicted patriarch is reconciled to life when he is convinced of the benevolent purposes of God in it. There is not a minute explanation of the meaning of every loss, but instead there is such a supreme consciousness of God's presence and goodness that the mind in joyful acquiescence ceases its questionings and the will its rebellion.

It will hardly be disputed that the spiritual insight and literary power of the Old Testament reaches its culmination in the latter part of the book of Isaiah, and that in the pathetic and strangely beautiful fifty-third chapter the inspiration of the prophet attains its highest point.

The great Prophet of the Exile has pondered long on the old problems of redemption and suf-

---

[1] Job xlii, 5.

fering, and his explanation is so startling that no one will believe his report. Suffering, he declares, is more than a penalty upon wrong-doing, it is more even than a permitted test of character,—it is one of God's chief instruments in redemption. It pleases him to bruise his Servant that through his stripes others may be healed. It was an epochal day in the world's religious history when the truth was uttered that vicarious suffering is one of God's elect and honored methods in salvation.

In the fervor of his utterance the prophet shows the cause which gives to the Sufferer profound peace in the furnace of his afflictions.

> "But Jehovah had purposed to bruise him,
> Had laid on him sickness;
> So if his life should offer guilt-offering,
> A seed he should see, he should lengthen his days.
> And the purpose of Jehovah by his hand should prosper,
> From the travail of his soul shall he see,
> By his knowledge be satisfied." [1]

The glory of the result reconciled the Servant to the process. Insight into the significance of his troubles took away every murmur. If he saw it was God's hand which held the cup to his lips, he could drink it.

This is certainly true teaching. We can be reconciled to life in its severest aspects if we are confident that the disasters are not meaningless, and that the valley of weeping can be made a

[1] Isaiah liii, 10, 11.

place of springs. All that we need to endure any tribulation is either the perception that it issues in a worthy result or the firm conviction that it is wisely ordered and that good will come out of evil.

We shall mention but one more Old Testament passage. In the Seventeenth Psalm the writer represents himself as beset with calamities, yet he knows that God is just. He does not ask for wealth or prosperity, but that in righteousness he may behold God's face. This beatific vision which comes to the soul in its most luminous moments is ample satisfaction for the losses and afflictions of life.

Modern writers are constantly referring to this ceaseless struggle of the sensitive soul with the grim facts of the world. They differ from the ancients more in forms of expression and method of approach than in their essential conclusions. John Addington Symonds gives a most noble description of the tortuous path by which a spirit, gifted with literary insight and steeped in modern scientific thought, finally found a satisfying faith which gave rest to his soul and girded his will with sufficient strength to fight life's battle with joy. Having lost the belief of his earlier years, he was advised by Comte to sit down contentedly and live without God. This he could not do. First the hymn of Cleanthes, suggesting the moral attitude of willing submission to universal law, gave to him a groundwork for a new faith. The reading of Marcus Aurelius and Goethe led him to believe that a religion which he called the religion of "cosmic enthusiasm" was the only one compatible with the agnosticism forced upon a candid mind. "Nothing but the bare thought of a God-penetrated universe, and of myself as an essential part of it, . . . satisfied me as a possible object of worship. When this thought flooded me, and filled the inmost fibres of my sentient being, I discovered that I was almost at rest about birth and death, and moral duties, and the problem of immortality. These were the world's affairs, not mine. Having lost the consolations of faith in redemption through Christ, and all that pertains thereto, I had gained in exchange this, that I could —

> lay myself upon the knees
> Of Doom, and take my everlasting ease."

Then a copy of Walt Whitman's "Leaves of Grass" came in his way. Here he found the same essential faith. Especially did he feel that this religion of "cosmic enthusiasm" was lived by the distinguished scientists of his day. "They threw themselves upon the world and God with simple self-devotion, . . . casting the burden of results upon *that* or *him* who called them into being, standing unterrified, at ease, before time, space, circumstance, and any number of sidereal systems."[1]

[1] *Life of John Addington Symonds*, by H. F. Brown, pp. 323 ff.

Whitman's reconciliation with life was due to the same mystical experience. His strong expression of faith is familiar.

"I believe in you, my soul . . .
Loafe with me on the grass, loose the stop from your throat ; . . .
Only the lull I like, the hum of your valved voice.
I mind how once we lay, such a transparent summer morning. . . .
Swiftly arose and spread around me the peace and knowledge
    that pass all the argument of the earth,
And I know that the hand of God is the promise of my own,
And I know that the spirit of God is brother of my own,
And that all the men ever born are also my brothers and the
    women my sisters and lovers,
And that a kelson of the creation is love."

In a soberer way he has elsewhere expressed the same thought. "There is apart from mere intellect, in the make-up of every superior human identity, a wondrous something that realizes without argument, frequently without what is called education (though I think it is the goal and apex of all education deserving the name), an intuition of the absolute balance in time and in space, of the whole of this multifariousness, this revel of fools, and incredible make-believe and general unsettledness, we call the world; a soul-sight of that divine clue and unseen thread which holds the whole congeries of things, all history and time, and all events, however trivial, however momentous, like a leashed dog in the hand of the hunter. Of such soul-sight and root-centre for the mind mere optimism explains only the surface."

[1] Poem entitled *Song of Myself*.
[2] Quoted in James's *The Varieties of Religious Experience*, p. 396.

This "soul-sight" of the unseen thread running through all events, without which great poetry is impossible, has received an equally strong utterance in Milton. At the close of "Samson Agonistes" the chorus exclaims: —

> "All is best, though we oft doubt,
> What th' unsearchable dispose
> Of highest wisdom brings about,
> And ever best found in the close."

While Whittier in a moment of lofty spiritual exaltation wrote the "Eternal Goodness," in which the whole philosophy of his reconciliation with life and all its apparent blighting cruelties burst forth into sweetest music.

> "I know not what the future hath
> Of marvel or surprise,
> Assured alone that life and death
> His mercy underlies.
>
> . . . . . .
>
> And so beside the Silent Sea
> I wait the muffled oar;
> No harm from Him can come to me
> On ocean or on shore.
>
> I know not where His islands lift
> Their fronded palms in air;
> I only know I cannot drift
> Beyond His love and care."

This mood, which was not exceptional, but reveals his habitual attitude toward life, was again voiced in "My Birthday."

> "I grieve not with the moaning wind
> As if a loss befell;

> Before me, even as behind,
> God is, and all is well.

> "His light shines on me from above,
> His low voice speaks within, —
> The patience of immortal love
> Outwearying mortal sin."

We would not imply that this is the only or even the characteristic mood of the literary seers and prophets of to-day. Some shout out the old stoical defiance : —

> "It matters not how strait the gate,
> How charged with punishments the scroll;
> I am the master of my fate,
> I am the captain of my soul."

Others advocate the outworn Epicurean prescription to lick the honey of life and forget the dragon at the bottom of the pit and the mice gnawing the roots of the tree of life. But the authors quoted show the only method of reconciliation with the whole of life. Their "rapturous espousal of the universe," "cosmic enthusiasm," or trust in the "Eternal Goodness" is the only solution which will meet all the exigencies of our experience and at the same time be an unfailing joy to the heart and strength to the will.

PART II

I

DEDUCTIONS

There is no principle involved in the atonement that is not included in its essence in the most sacred relations between man and man. — PHILLIPS BROOKS.

I am striving to bring the God which is in me into harmony with the God which is in the Universe. — PLOTINUS.

No true thinker dissents when the process of history is defined as reconciliation. — T. T. MUNGER.

CHAPTER I

DEDUCTIONS

Sin, Retribution, Forgiveness.

HAVING taken so extensive a journey among the masterpieces of literature, where we have found not merely individual opinion crystallized, but the aspirations and philosophy of great epochs given imperishable form, the profitable task remains of summarizing the knowledge gained. Then will come the greater work of deducing a generalization from the facts ascertained and systematized.

The different characteristics of sin which have appealed to various authors afford an engaging study. The view one takes of sin is conditioned by his conception of God. Homer, to whom the Supreme is the sum of all forces both good and evil, portrays sin as a blind following of impulse. This folly is often a spell sent by the gods, from which one does not escape until his eyes are opened. The immediate consequences are the defilement of the wrong-doer and the woe falling indiscriminately on both innocent and guilty. The defilement of sin is a permanent possession of religious thought. The forms in which it has appeared are protean: the lustral washing of the ancients, the Purgatory of the Catholic Church, Daniel O'Connell refusing to uncover in the presence of his Maker the hand which had killed a man in a duel, Hawthorne's quaint story of "The Minister's Black Veil" are illustrations.

Æschylus and Sophocles, while touching upon the stain of sin, are chiefly concerned with its continuous and widespread results. Sin taints the blood for generations; it disturbs the equilibrium of an inexorable moral system and evokes a frightful reprisal, destroying the innocent with the guilty. Dante affirms that spiritual blindness is sin's chief characteristic. "We have come," says Virgil, "to the place where I told thee that thou shalt see the woeful people who have lost the good of the understanding."[1] These stricken souls could not see God's justice, truth, and goodness shining through and giving significance to the untoward events of life. The issue of sin as portrayed in Lucifer is hideous and benumbed selfishness. In Milton's "Paradise Lost" sin is born of pride, erects a pandemonium of lawlessness, and degenerates into serpentine cunning and reptilian character. Shakespeare's Iago is crafty, morally blind, and contemptible. As we have already seen, the different characteristics of sin in Dante, Shakespeare, and Milton cannot be judged by the same standards. Milton portrays

[1] *Inferno*, iii.

sin as it was in the beginning, fair, resourceful, challenging our admiration; Shakespeare depicts it as it appears now in human shape, a worldly thing, mean, havoc-making, malignant; Dante lifts the curtain upon its final condition of foolish, sodden, repulsive monstrosity, without a redeeming trait.

About the certainty of retribution there is perfect unanimity. Nemesis follows hard after every transgressor. How one blind moment of folly blights the life of the individual, and spreads its leprosy from the individual to the family, and from the family to the state, this is a constant theme. There is no uncertainty here. The retribution of sin is sure, swift, terrible, casting far its poisoned net and entangling sinner and saint, the mature and the unborn in its fearful toils. The interpreters of the spiritual world are one in their vision of the reality of the moral order and the certainty of its recoil whenever it is disturbed by sin. The prophets of every age, country, and religion see eye to eye in this matter; they all speak the same warning. It has been felicitously said that the frontispiece of every one of George Eliot's works might fittingly be a pair of scales and a sword. The same symbol would serve for all the world's literary masterpieces. The sure movement of the scales and the flash of the sword are seen in them all.

In the unfolding of the principles upon which

forgiveness is won, our authors bring to light some facts well worthy of consideration. We are surprised to note their unanimity in declaring that the chief restraint upon the sinner in his downward course is a revelation of the consequences of his wrong. The religious mind, under the tuition of modern theology, has been taught to believe that the manifestation of the divine love in Christ is the supreme power in awakening a dead conscience; and the discovery that the force of declared love is almost entirely neglected in the masterpieces gives us cause for reflection. Achilles is cured of his obstinacy only when he sees the widespread slaughter of the Greeks; Œdipus knows his fault in the plague that lights upon Thebes; it is because Dante finds himself in a dark wood that he follows Reason and walks the upward way; Shakespeare kindles the fires of remorse when the guilty soul beholds the havoc of its iniquities; Milton depicts Adam as coming to a realization of his disobedience through a knowledge of the curse which is to fall on him and on his race. Arthur Donnithorne perceives that his sin is more than a slight infirmity when Hetty is charged with murder. The prodigal son comes to himself when he eats with swine.

The quickening into life of a conscience dead in trespasses and sins must not be confused with the enkindling of a sense of personal guilt.

The latter is quite another experience, and is originated in a very different way. It came to Dante as he stood before the stern face of Beatrice; it came to the prodigal when he saw himself in the light of his father's forgiveness and love; it comes to the Christian as he measures himself by the holiness of Christ. Love opens the eyes of the transgressor to the consequences of sin, not first of all to its own glories. The preaching of God's compassion may give to the awakened conscience a keener sense of personal guilt; but something quite different arouses a dead conscience to activity.

The great authors are one also in their conviction that there are certain conditions to be fulfilled before the old relationships can be resumed between those who have been alienated. Their unanimous testimony is beautifully summarized and symbolized in Dante's three steps leading to the gate of justification. There must be contrition, confession, satisfaction.

That pardon is impossible without repentance needs no argument. The guilty soul must be truly sorry for the wrong done, and turn from the evil in genuine contrition of spirit. Confession is the natural outgrowth of full penitence. A man determined upon thorough righteousness wishes to be known in his true character. He will wish the light to penetrate him and his deeds. He will be honest with himself, with the world, and with God. While the spiritual necessity of confession is generally recognized, it finds its most important emphasis in Dante and Hawthorne.

There is substantial agreement also that all possible satisfaction must be rendered to those who are injured in order to restore a perfect harmony. How the breach is filled up with satisfactory deeds has received many interpretations. If complete reparation is possible, then it must be made. Agamemnon must restore to the priest his daughter, and give back Briseis to Achilles. But most sins are so subtle and far-reaching that man cannot undo the evil he has done. His resources are pitifully inadequate for reparation. Forgiveness then depends upon the magnanimity of the one who has been wronged; it is not purchased, but is an act flowing out of a benignant nature; yet this free pardon is something more than a gush of good-natured impulse. Invariably it is a righteous act, in perfect accord with the requirements of moral law. As one turns the pages of Scripture and literature with the thought of the essential nature of forgiveness in mind, interest changes to wonder and wonder passes into the profound conviction that one is confronting an elemental truth on perceiving that every genuine pardon of transgression is so given that sin becomes hateful and the sanctity of the moral order of the world is revealed in its majesty and attractiveness. To this there is no exception. Forgiveness, to be genuine, must be so bestowed that moral obligations receive no diminution. The many forms in which this intuitive belief is expressed add impressiveness to the unanimity of the testimony. In Dante the sanctity of the eternal justice is maintained by the infliction of a penalty equivalent to the enormity of the sin, Christ bearing the eternal retribution and sinners the temporal pains. Thus God makes the scales to balance ere he forgives. In "Œdipus Tyrannus," sufferings not commensurate, but adequate to demonstrate the inviolability of the divine decrees, are inflicted. Æschylus presents another phase of satisfaction when he describes Orestes, a righteous man, enduring vicariously the consequences of the transgressions of others and by obedience and sorrow setting at rest the Furies of retributive justice. This is still more strongly asserted in the remarkable passage at the close of " Prometheus Bound:"—

> "Do not look
> For any end, moreover, of this curse,
> Or ere some god appear to accept thy pangs
> On his own head vicarious, and descend
> With unreluctant step the darks of hell
> And gloomy abysses around Tartarus."[1]

In the case of some of the authors whom we have investigated, the point of view shifts from the government of God to the conscience of the

[1] E. B. Browning's trans.

individual. The moral order without is reflected by the moral sense within, and the writer deals with the problem of so declaring forgiveness that the conscience of neither the forgiver nor the forgiven shall suffer offense. Pardon is still emphasized as righteous, and the attention is turned from the satisfaction of the law to the satisfaction of moral instincts and judgment.

Adam Bede is a just man. He cannot readily forgive Arthur Donnithorne for the betrayal of Hetty. What is best in his nature is aroused and clamant. His indignation is true and righteous. Yet when he sees the furrows of sorrow on Arthur's face and recognizes how completely the one who has injured him is bringing forth fruits meet for repentance, his wrath is allayed, and he forgives to the best of his ability.

King Arthur's love for Guinevere was holy. Its very purity made him shrink with greater horror from the shame of his queen. His devotion was not so slight a thing that it could by any possibility overlook moral distinctions, but the queen's overwhelming contrition quenched the flaming Sinai of his indignation. Her repentance made possible holy love; his love could be both pitying and righteous, and he could say,—

"Lo! I forgive thee, as Eternal God Forgives."

Neither Guinevere nor Arthur Donnithorne would have felt forgiven had each not realized that the new attitude towards the past, the sorrow, penitence, and effort to undo the evil so far as possible, was a real homage to the laws of morality which had been broken. The principle of propitiation to conscience, to the holiness of love, as a condition of forgiveness, is clearly recognized by George Eliot, Tennyson, Hosea in his treatment of Gomer, and Hawthorne in his portrayal of how Hester Prynne won her way to the forgiveness of the stern Puritan community by meeting the demands of their rigorous consciences. Æschylus, Sophocles, and Dante are interested in the satisfaction of the moral government of God; Hosea, Hawthorne, George Eliot, and Tennyson call attention to the inner satisfaction or propitiation of outraged conscience and holiness.

Our investigations justify these conclusions. Sin is forgivable. But no matter how earnestly the injured one wishes to wipe out the offense, there are certain conditions which must be fulfilled. The one who is forgiven must have an adequate apprehension of his transgression; that is, he must know and be known for what he is by all the persons concerned. He must also be genuinely repentant, and, to the extent of his ability, make reparation for the evil committed. But forgiveness, to be real, must be righteous; it must in no way minimize sin, or diminish the sanctions of the moral order, or offend the holiness of love or the instincts of conscience. The authors we have studied are unanimous in this, although they differ according to their temperament and training in their teaching of the methods by which law and conscience are satisfied.

Invariably, also, both in literature and in life, the austerity and authority of the moral law are revealed by the sufferings which the infraction of moral relationships entails. The sufferings may be merited or vicarious, but they are an indispensable condition of forgiveness. Without the shedding of blood there is no remission. The moral order always makes known its violation by the penalty it exacts, and the resulting woe reveals the authority of the ethical world.

We are warranted, therefore, in affirming that if there is a disposition on the part of the injured one to forgive, and genuine repentance in the heart of the wrong-doer, there is no obstacle to complete pardon, provided the mercy is so granted and accepted that the true nature of the wrong is understood by both parties, and the sanctities of moral obligation receive no weakening.

Reconciliation.

Reconciliation is a larger question than forgiveness. It includes forgiveness, and then stretches out over new experiences and needs. The penitent may know that he is forgiven; but can he forgive himself? Pardon does not perforce make him complacent with his past. His will may have gone wholly over to the good; his heart may rest in a sweet sense of forgiveness; but his conscience may still be a flaming pillar of remorse, and his memory a Gehenna of torment. Forgiveness is only an element in reconciliation. Forgiveness need concern but two persons, while reconciliation may demand the reorganization of the universe. Forgiveness does not wipe out the fact of sin, nor the memory of it, nor its consequences. There can be no unshadowed and perfectly restored relationships unless the memories of both the offender and the offended one can dwell at peace beside the forgiven offense. The stricken mind of Macbeth instinctively felt that his horror-crammed memory presented the greatest obstacle to peace. He cries to his physician:

> "Canst thou not minister to a mind diseas'd,
> Pluck from the memory a rooted sorrow,
> Raze out the written troubles of the brain,
> And with some sweet oblivious antidote
> Cleanse the stuff'd bosom of that perilous stuff
> Which weighs upon the heart?"[1]

Milton's Adam may believe his sin to be forgiven, but his personal deliverance is of slight moment. How can he dwell in celestial light, with a blackened memory and the knowledge that his sin is ranging on in ever-increasing destructiveness through the generations of men? Job acknowledges no need of forgiveness. He is willing to

[1] Macbeth, V, sc. III.

maintain his integrity in the presence of his Maker, yet he is reconciled to neither past nor present, to neither man nor God. King Arthur forgives Guinevere, but he clearly affirms that reconciliation is at present impossible. Hereafter, when certain conditions have been fulfilled, they may be brought into perfect reunion before High God. Certainly the queen is not at peace with herself.

Many of the seers of literature do not hesitate to affirm that perfect reconciliation is impossible.

> "The moving Finger writes; and having writ
> Moves on; not all your Piety nor Wit
> Shall lure it back to cancel half a Line,
> Nor all your Tears wash out a word of it."[1]

An irrevocable past throws a perpetual shadow. It may be forgiven, but not joyously acquiesced in. The reader will recall Adam Bede's pathetic statement: "There's a sort of wrong that can never be made up for."

But many of the authors we have examined recognized a principle which changes tragedy into happiness, and by a divine alchemy transmutes remorse into peace, and profound sorrows into songs of rejoicing.

Dante wrote the Divine Comedy instead of the Divine Tragedy, because the most embittered life may have a happy ending. The soul may experience a Lethe which can "cleanse the stuff'd

[1] *Rubáiyát* of Omar Khayyám, lxxi.

bosom of that perilous stuff which weighs upon the heart." It has its Eunoë of reinvigoration, and it will finally raise its look unto the Eternal Goodness, and in beholding him have peace.

When Shakespeare retired from the stage, he indicated in "The Tempest" those conceptions of life in its ultimate meanings which enabled him to look without disquiet on the sufferings and wrongs which he had experienced. He represents Prospero as reconciled to his enemies and with tranquil mind looking back over the years. The enchanter can so readily forget all hardships and forgive all wrongs, because his unobstructed power has brought good out of evil. His realization of the final good compensates for the severity of the process. Had Miranda been ruined by the lust of Caliban, and Prospero's own life been hopelessly crippled by the malignity of his foes, he might have forgiven them and submitted to his cruel lot with composed resignation; but genuine reconciliation, either with the past or with the providential order of the world, would have been impossible. Reconciliation resulted from the victory which his good-will won over all evil. The good had conquered, and had set the wrong right. The wound caused by sin was healed. This was the basis of his acquiescence in the experiences of life and the source of his satisfaction. What reconciled Prospero was also the reconciliation of the Master who created him. I do not think we overstate the truth when we assert that Shakespeare's belief in "some soul of goodness in things evil," a goodness which subdues evil and makes it minister to a higher well-being, was the ground of his own contentment. Milton affirms that for Adam there was no painless blessedness until from a high mountain he saw how God was to display the splendor of redeeming grace through his transgression, while the plinth upon which the finely wrought superstructure of " Paradise Regained " is reared is the doctrine that Christ's victorious life is the compensation for the sin of the world and the open gate through which all men may pass to everlasting felicity.

Job lays his hand upon his mouth when he hears God's answer out of the whirlwind of his troubles, and is satisfied that His way has been true and righteous; Isaiah's Suffering Servant is satisfied with the travail of his soul when he sees his seed and the pleasure of the Lord prospering at his hand; and the Psalmist knows he cannot be satisfied or reconciled until he sees the Lord face to face. King Arthur could forgive Guinevere out of the greatness of his love, but reconciliation was impossible so long as the stain of her sin was upon her, and his mortal eyes could behold only red ruin and the breaking up of laws. But his faith and hope reached beyond, and he intimates that when they meet before High God, her own sin conquered, and the divine work in the world perfected, then he can take her to himself in shadowless reconciliation.

Through these many witnesses we have a principle of reconciliation very clearly attested. Perfect accord between God and man, or between injured and injurer, or between man and his past and present, depends upon the supremacy of Good over evil. This triumphant goodness may be realized, as by Prospero in "The Tempest," or it may be seen in vision, as in Dante, Milton, Isaiah's Suffering Servant, and the writer of the Seventeenth Psalm; or accepted by faith, as by Whittier, Symonds, Whitman; but the healing of the hurt of sin, the reparation wrought by victorious goodness, is essential to reconciliation. If for the consequences of an evil deed there were no remedy, if crime had a perpetual triumph, if no compensations came to undo sin's terrible effects, then a soul might rise to forgiveness, but not to any state of mind that could be called reconciliation. Glad acquiescence in the experiences of life, or in the ways of God, or in an irrevocable past, depends upon the actual conquest of evil by the good or the perception of that final triumph by the eye of faith. Repentance and pardon may restore sundered relationships, but something more is needed for that peace and joy which are the promised rewards of those who have struggled through sin to holiness. Reconciliation is forgiveness plus that repose of the mind which can only come through an unalterable conviction that evil is either restrained or in God's wise providence ministers to a final good.

The reality of sin, the certainty of retribution, the impossibility of forgiveness unless the authority of the moral law is maintained and the conscience satisfied, and the possibility of reconciliation when the compensations of the good, either realized or seen by faith, overbalance the losses inflicted by evil, — these are the fundamental teachings of literature.

II

POETS AND THEOLOGIANS

No great writer represents the whole of Christianity in its application to life. But I think that almost every great writer, since the religion of Jesus touched the leading races, has helped to reveal some new aspect of its beauty, to make clear some new secret of its sweet reasonableness, or to enforce some new lesson of its power. — HENRY VAN DYKE.

The cardinal truth of a great reparation in behalf of mankind is imbedded in the teachings of the Bible. It has entered as a vital element into the Christian experience of the ages; it pervades the hymns and prayers of the church from the apostolic days until now; it is involved essentially in the Eucharist. If history is worth anything as a witness, the result of discarding this doctrine will be to deprive the gospel of the essential element of its power over the consciences and hearts of men. — GEORGE P. FISHER.

CHAPTER II

POETS AND THEOLOGIANS

WHEN we take the principles which we have observed and classified, and apply them to our study of the problem of reconciliation between God and man, we come immediately upon a very interesting and convincing parallelism. It has often been charged that the theologians have woven their theories of the atonement out of distorted views of God, poor exegesis, and mistaken conceptions of the nature of the divine government. Doomed by their unnatural origin, these dogmas are malformed and unworthy children of the brain, unfit to be domiciled. On the contrary, it can be shown that every interpretation of the cross which has entered vitally into the life of the Christian Church rests upon a principle which has received recognition by some world-famous mind in literature. Every great theory of the atonement can be matched by a story of reconciliation embodied in some drama, poem, or work of fiction which has lived because in a form of beauty it has presented an elemental truth. Over against every prominent expounder of the atonement is a poet or a novelist who caught the same vision and proclaimed the same essential verity. The evidential value of this fact is of superlative importance. It proves that the chief expositions of reconcilement between God and man have come out of the burning heart of humanity, and are not unwarranted conclusions of minds still in the twilight of religious knowledge. It proves that widely received and regnant dogmas of the atonement, although encrusted with inadequate ideas of God and false logic, contain an important germ of truth upon which men's minds instinctively laid hold and were nourished thereby.

Let us briefly glance at the fundamental agreements between poets and theologians. The New Testament contains no elaborated statements of the significance of the work of Christ. It teaches the fact of the reconciliation of men to God through Christ, and uses bold metaphors to impress the different aspects of salvation, but the writers stood too near the stupendous events and freshly revealed truths to speculate about their relationship.

The Patristic doctrine of how Christ saves men from sin was an expiatory theory which was more fully expounded in the Middle Ages. Along with this was developed the strange teaching, founded upon the literal interpretation of a New Testament metaphor[1] that Christ was given to Satan as a ransom. As this conception is not based upon an instinct, but upon a misinterpre-

[1] Col. ii, 15 ; Heb. ii, 14.

tation of Scripture, we do not find it in the poets. It expresses no other truth than that through Christ we attain liberty.

With Anselm's epoch-making book, *Cur Deus Homo*, published in 1098, we have the first thorough examination of the necessity demanding the death of Christ, and an attempted explanation of the full significance of that tragedy. Sin is here set forth as a dishonor inflicted upon God, — it is an affront to the divine majesty. God's infinite perfections require that the sin be punished. The sinner must pay this debt which he owes to the divine honor, or suffer the penalty. He is powerless to cancel his obligation; God only can do it. Hence the necessity of a God-Man, one who is the gift of God's love, yet truly man's representative. The yielding up of Christ's life was a free gift, and as this life was of more value than all worlds, its voluntary sacrifice was more valuable than sin is heinous, and the offering of it rendered due reverence to the divine character.

The idea of sin as a dishonor to the gods was a familiar thought to Homer. In the first book of the Iliad, the offended Apollo avenges the insult offered to his priest by sending a pestilence upon the Greeks. Sacrifices were made to him that honor might atone for the dishonor. What in Homer is an uninterpreted instinct is developed in Æschylus into a reasoned philosophy very similar to that of Anselm. In the Orestiad, Agamemnon violates the sanctity of the home by slaying his daughter. The dishonored family vindicates itself by the murder of the king. The crime is an offense against the state, which asserts its rights by the death of Clytemnestra. Sin is an affront which demands punishment or homage to the offended dignity. Must the destructive reaction between family and state go on forever? How can atonement be made? The answer is found in the character, official position, and sufferings of Orestes; even as Anselm found his solution in the character, nature, and sufferings of Christ. Orestes is a righteous man. As he has obeyed Apollo, his sufferings are supererogatory. Moreover, he is both the child of Agamemnon and Clytemnestra, and a prince in the state. Representing both parties, he can be a mediator between them, and his woes, being unmerited, give satisfactory honor to all offended rights. While the materials and scenery of the Greeks differ widely from those used by the mediæval saint, they and he are interpreting the same essential instincts and philosophy of life.

Anselm does not dwell on the extent of the Saviour's sufferings nor on his death as a substituted penalty, but this conception naturally grows out of his thought, and was seized upon and elaborated by Aquinas and the Schoolmen. They taught that the vicarious work of Christ was the real and absolute equivalent for that which the transgressor owes to God and his justice. Sin is a debt which Christ and his redeemed pay to the full. The scales balance, and perfect justice is done.

The poet who lends his authority to this system of cosmic accuracy is Dante. From his temperament his mind naturally gravitated toward a philosophy of exact and even-handed justice. He is conspicuously the poet of the justice of God, and while no writer has excelled him in vivid and powerful portrayal of that divine love which penetrates all things, yet it is not a lawless affection; always and everywhere it works in accordance with strictest and minutest justice. Sin, in his conception, is a breach in the moral order; full satisfaction must be made. It wounds the character; the scars must be completely healed. Christ in his agonies took upon himself the eternal penalties of sin. He might have "paid it all," so that the penitent would have nothing to do but enjoy the benefits of this salvation; but this would not have been wise. Therefore the souls in purgatory expiate the temporal consequences of their own sin. "Where sin makes void, they fill up for evil pleasures with just penalties."[1] The penitent spirit has something to do for his own salvation. While by baptism he enters into the benefits of Christ's

---

[1] *Paradiso*, vii, 82, 84.

work for him, he has a satisfaction to render for his sins committed after baptism. The purgatorial punishments have a double efficacy; they accomplish a satisfaction to the moral order and are purifying to the penitent.

Yet pain is not the only way of cleansing the soul and satisfying righteousness. In ante-Purgatory Dante asked Virgil how intercessory prayer could bend the decree of heaven. The reply was: "For the top of judgment veils not itself, because a fire of love may, in one instant, fulfill that which he who is stationed here must satisfy."[1] That is, love can take the place of punishment without weakening justice. Prayers and the good deeds of the innocent are accepted in lieu of the expiatory punishment of the guilty.

All this seems mediæval enough, and far removed from our modern habits of thought. However, it has for us great evidential value. A theology which has held a commanding position in the Roman Catholic Church for centuries, winning the cordial assent of many of the best minds of Europe, and has been made fundamental in the song of one of the three greatest singers of the world, rests upon a sure instinct of our natures. That instinct is this: There can be no forgiveness where love does not work in such a way as to satisfy the strictest demands of conscience and meet every requirement of

[1] *Purgatorio*, vi, 37–59.

perfect repentance. Forgiveness is a holy act, and it cannot be real unless its holiness is manifested.

Many minds in the Middle Ages to whom the penal satisfaction ideas of Anselm and Aquinas seemed too mechanical found relief in the acceptation theory of Duns Scotus, who held that God graciously accepted Christ's sufferings as satisfactory. The pains of Calvary were not the equivalent of those demanded by a broken law, but God received them as sufficient to meet all the demands of offended majesty.

The transition from the severe justice maintained by Aquinas to the equity advocated by Duns Scotus is reflected in literature by the change from Æschylus to Sophocles. In the latter, while the austerity of the moral universe is set forth with marvelous power, there is less insistence upon the idea of blood for blood. The sufferings of Œdipus, though due to a violated law, are not carefully weighed in a balance, but accomplish his purification, and finally win the compassion of the gods. This failure to emphasize the exactitude of justice may be explained by the different story which Sophocles dramatized; still the more probable reason is that his temperate mind was disinclined to trace an equation between sin and suffering.

Another widely influential theory of the atonement is that originally propounded by Grotius, the eminent jurist of the seventeenth century. We are subjects, he maintained, under the moral government of God. A governor can remit the penalties of the law, provided the end for which the punishment was ordained is fulfilled. This end is the preservation of the sanctity of the law and the prevention of future transgression. The death of Christ honors the moral law by revealing the heinous nature of sin and God's hatred of it. The work of Christ, by maintaining the majesty of righteousness and deterring man from sin, meets all the ends of the penalty. This conception is still in much favor both in its form and substance. It is also much protested against by many as not sufficiently recognizing the fundamental truth that we are children in a Father's house rather than subjects of a king. Granting that the form of the statement is not in accordance with our modes of expression, yet a theory so influential must have a substratum of truth. In the providential government of the universe the purpose of penalty appears to be to restrain from sin, and to interpret and vindicate the nature of things. It cannot be remitted unless in some other way the moral order is so interpreted and vindicated that man is restrained from transgression. There can be no forgiveness in which the majesty of the moral law is not upheld. With this principle we have grown very familiar in our investigation, — it is amply recognized in the great

Greek writers. Homer's heroes must show due reverence to the gods before the penalties are remitted. Orestes honors the Erinnyes before they cease their fierce pursuit. Only a god suffering vicariously can release Prometheus. Œdipus must bear his load of woe that the inviolability of the structural laws of the world may be revealed. The Greek dramatists laid an emphasis as insistent and as well considered as that of Grotius on the impossibility of remitting punishment unless the purposes of punishment are met. In the working out of their stories Homer and Æschylus distinctly recognize the principles for which the Dutch theologian contends.

McLeod Campbell, in his devout and soul-stirring book entitled "The Nature of the Atonement," uttered in theology the truth we hear from Hawthorne in literature. Campbell asserted that all the demands of a broken law were met either by penalty or by repentance. An adequate repentance of sin and acknowledgment of the divine holiness satisfies all the demands of righteous government, for goodness is revered, sin detested, and both are known in their true nature. Christ, as our high priest, took upon his heart a full consciousness of the sin of the world, and made complete confession of it before God. Humanity by faith enters into the consciousness of Christ, and looks upon sin with his abhorrence and upon righteousness with his loyalty. The place of confession in forgiveness was clearly recognized in Dante, who made it one of the three steps to justification, while, as we have seen, Hawthorne gives it conspicuous recognition.

The moral influence theory of the atonement is greatly in vogue to-day. As we often hear it expounded, it amounts to little more than this: God, in the life, sufferings, and death of Jesus Christ, so revealed his fatherly love and pity that men are persuaded to repentance and won to a life of rectitude and filial obedience. This makes Christ an actor and Calvary a spectacular performance. The voice both of literature and of experience is strongly against any such trifling and artificial conception of redemption. In all the authors we have studied, the sinner has been aroused by a knowledge of the consequences of his sin, and not by any vision of the glories of righteousness. The penalties of sin check the footsteps of the one going in the wrong way; the solicitations of love are effective after the sin has become abhorrent.

Horace Bushnell, who is perhaps the most powerful exponent of the so-called "moral influence theory," proclaims a much more virile and natural doctrine than that ordinarily taught. He sought to avoid any such dilutions of his teaching as have become current. Christ, he affirms, does more than reveal God's fatherly compassion; he is "the Moral Power of God upon us;" "he executes the remission by taking away the sin and dispensing the justification of life."

When our attention is turned toward this aspect of forgiveness, we think immediately of Bishop Bienvenu in "Les Misérables," conquering the vengeful soul of Jean Valjean by the subduing force of his goodness. In that celestial light the convict sees his fallen nature. Shakespeare, in "The Winter's Tale," but more definitely still in "The Tempest," touches upon Bushnell's principle. It is the goodness of Prospero that leads his enemies into a full repentance. He makes no dramatic exhibition of superior moral endowments; but the penalties he inflicts arouse their consciences, while the greatness of his nature tempers their minds to unwonted virtue.

The idea of propitiation has loomed large both in sacrificial systems and in theories of the atonement. The religious thought of the world has held that God is justly angry with sin. Before there can be abundant pardon this righteous indignation must be allayed. From the time the first victim was bound on an altar to appease an angry god to the publication of Bushnell's able work on "Forgiveness and Law," the propitiation idea has been influential in theology. It has also been conspicuous in literature. Propitiation by the suffering of both injured and injurer is strongly emphasized by Hosea, Hawthorne,

George Eliot, and Tennyson. It must be noted, however, that the propitiation which these authors portray is nothing legal or mechanical. The sufferings of Gomer, Hester Prynne, Arthur Donnithorne, and Guinevere are propitiatory to the injured because they reveal a new attitude of mind to old sins, and disclose a new and fairer nature being born out of an alien and rejected self. Suffering is demanded by the guilty ones themselves as the only suitable expression of the new temper of mind, and as an appropriate satisfaction to their own aroused feelings.

We must not press analogies too far, or be misled by words, yet I think we are strictly within the truth when we affirm that both poets and theologians have expressed — the former in the beauty of art, and the latter in the clear-cut statements of dogma — the same elemental principles. They agree that forgiveness is no easy matter, — a slight favor to be had for the asking. The conscience, which gives an immediate knowledge of the reality and grandeur of the ethical structure of the universe, and which thus knows sin and bears the burden of it, feels the inexorable demands of justice and cannot be satisfied with any forgiveness which ignores in the slightest degree the sanctity of the moral law. The warp and woof of all pardon, human and divine, must be righteous if forgiveness is to be genuine and permanent. The theologians have assumed the love of

God as the source of forgiveness for sin, but they have recognized that his love, however tender, was holy love. Pardoning mercy must in no way dim the lustre of holiness; it must not impair the authority of the moral imperatives. The religious feeling demands that God be both holy and merciful. The holiness in mercy has not been conceived as an obstacle to God's forgiveness, but it has been a constant problem to our understanding of the divine pardon. Sin and holiness must be known in their true nature, that forgiveness may be genuine. Anselm, Duns Scotus, Grotius note the fact that holiness and sin are known through suffering, while Campbell approaches the same truth by declaring that sin and holiness are best revealed in the consciousness of Christ, and by entering into that consciousness we are in a condition to be forgiven.

Many and rich have been the conceptions of forgiveness which have sprung from out humanity's needs, but they are all rooted and nourished in an instinct of justice. How can the injured one be just and merciful at the same time, is the age-long problem. When the relationship between God and man was the subject of thought, the question has been: How can God be just, and the justifier of the transgressor? The enigma has been approached from different points of view. Some have seen the governmental difficulties, others the necessity of appeasing the indignation which divine holiness must feel in the presence of sin, others have contemplated the difficulties from the standpoint of the offender, and shown that the guilty conscience cannot rest in a forgiveness that is not holy. Whatever the side of the problem touched, whatever the century in which the mind took thought of the theme, the conclusion was invariable that forgiveness must be in strict accord with fundamental righteousness; in its very going forth it must reveal the blackness of sin and unveil the august majesty of holiness.

The poets have felt the pressure of the same inexorable moral world, and have met its problems in much the same way.

The principles we have been discussing all deal with the problem of forgiveness; but *reconciliation* is a word of deeper significance, and covers a greater complexity of relations. To what extent do literature and theology harmonize in their teachings of the ways by which the wounds of sin are completely healed? The dogma of the atonement is but little discussed among us because the men of the past have done their work so well. It is a religious commonplace that God is ready to forgive, and that in Christ the nature of sin and the glories of holiness are so made manifest that whosoever is in Christ may be forgiven freely without lowering the sanctions of the divine justice. The phase of reconciliation which interests the modern man is not forgiveness, but adjustment to the facts of life. His struggle is to accept the universe. Reconciliation with life, or with God's providential dealings with him, engages him far more than the forgiveness of his sins.

Sometimes the reconciliation needs to be with the past, rather than with the conditions of the present. A Lethe for the memory is needed, a cleansing of an evil conscience, else life is a perpetual torment. Sometimes it is the future, with its portents of woe, to which we must adjust ourselves. But whether the source of trouble is a blackened memory, present misfortune, or future dread, reconciliation has always come through a faith in a goodness which is in all and over all. Dante found every murmur stilled in the beatific vision; Shakespeare trusted to the "soul of goodness in things evil;" Milton complained not at his blindness, because "all is best;" Whitman never forgot the luminous hour when he knew that "a kelson of the creation is love;" Whittier rested in the Eternal Goodness, and had no fear.

This method of reconciliation, as old as Job and as recent as Whittier, has always been recognized in the teachings of the Church. It found its crassest expression when the New England theologians declared that as the saints look over the battlements of heaven upon the damned smoking in torment their shouts of praise ascend to the throne of God! Their rejoicing is possible because through the smoke and the torture they behold the glory of the perfect righteousness of the Most High. This is but a scenic exaggeration of accepted truth. The pulpit has always affirmed that the way of peace is the way of submission. To accept God's will, to take life on the conditions he has assigned, to believe that all things are working for good, — this is a familiar teaching, yet it has never been made an essential part of the doctrine of the atonement. This stone rejected of the builders should be very near the head of the corner. How important it is we shall see in a following chapter. But that the victorious goodness of God has a prominent part in any tenet of reconciliation would seem to go without saying. That faith in the triumph of the divine will over all evil is essential to a Christian's reconciliation with the facts and forces of life is evident. Belief in the soul of goodness in things evil which ultimately conquers the evil, brings order out of chaos and light out of darkness, and makes mistakes, calamities, sins even, minister to well-being, — this is fundamental in experience, and ever recurring wherever reconciliation is touched upon in literature. What is so basic in thought and experience is not negligible in a gospel of reconciliation.

III

WHAT DID JESUS OF NAZARETH DO FOR THE FORGIVENESS OF OUR SINS?

Were the human Conscience, like human Prudence, the mere product of experience; were it the reflection of the world's opinion; were it given only for our temporal guidance without significance beyond; why should we not get rid of our sins as we do of our mistakes, — commit them and have done with them, — and leave no ghost behind? This is actually the approved wisdom of hard and driving men whose ethics are but the instruments of external work. But where there is a deeper insight, where the outer doing is looked upon as the symbol of the inner being, where affection, character, will, have any life and drama of their own, this discharge of old compunctions, this cheerful erasure of bankrupt accounts, is quite impossible. Only when evil is regarded as a transitory mishap, can it be thus forgot: once let the consciousness awake that it is disloyalty to the Spirit of eternal Holiness, and there is in this a conservative power which will forbid its awful shadow to depart. And hence, strange as it may seem, it is not the guilty who know the most of guilt; it is the pure, the lofty, the faithful, that are ever haunted by the sense of sin, and are compelled by it to throw themselves upon a love they never doubt yet cannot claim. . . . Why do you hear from a Fénelon words of humiliation that never escape a Richelieu? why are the prayers of prophets and hymns of saintly souls so pathetic in their penitence, so full of the plaintive music of baffled aspiration, like the cry of some bird with broken wing? It is because to them the truly infinite nature of holiness has revealed itself, and reveals itself the more, the higher they rise; because in its secret breathings to their hearts they recognize, not any romance of their own, but the communing Spirit of the Living God. . . . But if this be the meaning of our sense of sin, what hope, you will say, that it can ever leave us? Was it not the work of Christ to give us rest from the strife and sorrows of compunction? Yes: not, however, a rest within ourselves, as if we either ceased from sin or could see it with other or less saddened eyes; but a rest out of ourselves, a pure and perfect trust in Him whose spirit draws us from before and whose pity supports us from behind. — MARTINEAU.

CHAPTER III

WHAT DID JESUS OF NAZARETH DO FOR THE FORGIVENESS OF OUR SINS?

We now draw near the conclusion of our task. In the long, and we trust not uninteresting, journey we have taken among the masterpieces, we have come to the recognition of certain clear principles. Forgiveness and reconciliation are not unreal or impossible words. Given a disposition to pardon on the part of the offended one, certain conditions are essential to bring about perfect forgiveness: the guilty person must repent of his deed, but the repentance cannot be genuine if the nature of the offense is not adequately known. Contrition which has no clear apprehension of the nature of the deed done is no contrition at all. Not only must the criminal recognize the real nature of his fault, but he can have no sense of full forgiveness unless he is convinced that the one who grants the mercy does so with a knowledge of what the sin is and all that is involved in it. An adequate understanding of the offense forgiven, both by the offender and the offended, is indispensable to a thorough-going and satisfactory forgiveness. But the pardoning transaction takes place in a moral world which suffers no infringement of its solemn laws. Forgiveness must not only be merciful, it must be just. This principle looms up with commanding impressiveness in every great drama and work of fiction. Of unquestioned authority in literature, it has been equally conspicuous in theology. The burden resting upon the mind of every prominent interpreter of the atonement has been to show that God is just while justifying the sinner. The majesty of the moral law must not be diminished or its splendor dimmed by any act of mercy.

The necessity of not in any way rending the fabric of ethical obligation by the going forth of forgiveness is further emphasized by the fact that sin is recognized through an aroused conscience. The moral sense, once awakened, cannot be allayed by any method which comes short of satisfying its insistent demands. Forgiveness must be in harmony with the moral sentiments, or it is not forgiveness.

But forgiveness is not reconciliation. The latter is a far more comprehensive word. Complete reconciliation we have learned is impossible unless both the injured and the injurer see that good has come out of the evil done, or else have so strong a faith in an overruling Providence as to believe that the evil is caught up into God's redemptive purpose and will be made to serve his ends.

With these definite principles clearly in mind, we are prepared to ask the question: "How are men reconciled to God in Jesus Christ?" To follow the line of cleavage already traced we shall first inquire: "What did Jesus of Nazareth do for the forgiveness of our sins?" We shall then be prepared to press the further interrogation, "How are men reconciled to God through him?"

No sooner had Jesus ended his earthly life, and the belief in his resurrection taken possession of his disciples, than they began to preach remission of sins in his name. It was first proclaimed at Pentecost, and was a conspicuous message of the apostolic church. The Christ had died, and the reason he had submitted unto death was that repentance and remission of sins might be preached in his name. That ancient gospel is true. It has been attested by the experience of twenty centuries. It has been certified in many millions of lives. Whoever has come within the circle of Jesus' influence, and yielded to the spell of his personality, has felt the burden of his sin roll away. He has been saved both from the love of sin and from the power of sin; he has been profoundly convinced that God has forgiven him, and that he has come into a condition of unimpeded filial relationship. "His name shall be called Jesus," say the Scriptures, "for he shall save his people from their sins." His name is still called Jesus, because he does save his people from their sins.

When we analyze what the historical Jesus of Nazareth has done either to assure us of forgiveness of our sins, or to procure that forgiveness for us, his work resolves itself into the following achievements: —

(1) He aroused and deepened men's consciousness of God's moral character.

He did not reveal to them the existence of God. That had long been the fundamental article of the creeds. He did not declare God's nearness. In words of unsurpassed power the Psalmist had exclaimed: "Whither shall I go from thy spirit? or whither shall I flee from thy presence? If I ascend up into heaven, thou art there; if I make my bed in hell, behold, thou art there. If I take the wings of the morning and dwell in the uttermost parts of the sea; even there shall thy hand lead me, and thy right hand shall hold me." He was not the first to disclose the divine compassion. Centuries before his day the Psalmist had also declared: "Like as a father pitieth his children, so the Lord pitieth them that fear him." He did not first unfold the awful holiness of the Most High. "Be ye holy, for I am holy," was the structural thought of the Jewish law. What did Jesus do? He lived a life so unique in purity, power, and beauty that he intensified and made clear, just, and compelling our sense of the character of God.

A man must needs build his house out of the material he has at his command. The Esquimau within the Arctic Circle constructs his home of snow and ice ; the dweller in tropic lands employs the bamboo and palm tree. Each utilizes the material nature has given him knowledge of and power over. In the same way do we rear the structures in which our minds rest. We cannot put anything into our mental concepts which has not come into the circle of our consciousness. We build our thoughts and ideals out of the facts of experience. After Jesus of Nazareth had lived his life, a new and stupendous fact had come into human experience, — a new sense of God, a fresh and august conception of holiness, an impressive realization of the virility and beauty of compassion. This startling and luminous fact led men's minds upward. It clarified, enriched, enthroned their knowledge of God. Hitherto men had known God as he was disclosed in the energy and grandeur of nature. They understood him better as he was revealed in the person and words of his prophets, for the processes of history declare the moral attributes of the Eternal more clearly than the processes of nature. God manifests himself more fully in the spiritual nature of man than in the material world. The human soul is a higher revelation of God than the mountains or the stars. Humanity at its best is certainly God's highest possible revelation of himself, and man at his best is Jesus Christ. Those who come within the circle of Christ's influence by the spontaneous action of their minds must think of God through the light which he brings into their thoughts. What Jesus was in pity, sympathy, righteousness, serves to interpret what God is in his essential nature. The splendor of the qualities which the Master revealed on Calvary men must believe to be the outshining of the nature of the Most High. Humanity gets its most exalted notion of Deity through man at his best, and especially through the loftiest moments of the best man. Hence it is that on Calvary men have found the material out of which they have constructed their noblest thought of God. Or, in other words, it is by this method that God has made the supreme revelation of himself. The loftiest moments of the supreme man afford the most intimate knowledge of the heart of the Everlasting.

Having once known Jesus, men can no longer think of God as a relentless monarch, unforgiving unless propitiated by an holocaust of victims. They must enter into Jesus' consciousness of a Father who so loves the world that he sends his only begotten Son to redeem it. He loves men, not because they are noble and worthy, but because he is God! and it is the very glory of God to love men in their sins that he may save them from the bondage of evil. He is not an outraged Being who waits in sullen anger for the prodigal to return and allay his wrath, but he is a Father watching in solicitous love for the wanderers to come home. Like a good shepherd, he seeks the one who has gone astray, even at cost to himself; like the housewife, searching every nook and corner for a piece of silver, he searches for the lost; he stands at the door and knocks; he compels the outcasts to come to the feast. This is the nature of Jesus; it is also the nature of God, for the Son doeth whatsoever he seeth the Father do.

After this revelation in Jesus Christ, all notions of teasing God into an attitude of forgiveness by prayers, or sacrifices, or elaborate ceremonial, must vanish from Christian thought. It is God who makes the offering; it is God who presents the sacrifices; it is God who solicits men. After Jesus' sacrificial life and death religious thought must assume as its fundamental postulate the good will of God toward men. It is he who takes the initiative in the atonement, and not man. Indeed, so firmly established did the idea become, that the grimmest theologian took it for granted. Behind the bloodiest and most austere theories of penal satisfaction or legal substitution was the presupposition that it was God who opened the way and provided the means of atonement. Calvin quotes these words of Augustine with entire approval: "God did not begin to love us when we were reconciled to him by the blood of his Son; but he loved us before the creation of the world, that we might be his children, together with his only begotten Son, even before we had any existence. Therefore our reconciliation by the death of Christ must not be understood as if he reconciled us to God that God might begin to love those whom he had before hated; but we are reconciled to him who already loved us and with whom we were at enmity on account of sin."[1] In another place Augustine writes: "Unless the Father had been already appeased, would he have delivered up his own Son, not sparing him for us? But I see that the Father loved us also before, not only before the Son died for us, but before he created the world."[2]

The older theologians are often accused of representing Christ as creating good will in God toward men. The only ground for such charges lies in the artificial way in which they present Christ as upholding the divine justice in forgiveness. They placed the emphasis on the work of Christ in removing the obstacles to forgiveness; but they assumed a good will in God eager to

[1] Institutes, bk. 11, ch. xvi.
[2] Quoted by Professor Stevens in *The Christian Doctrine of Salvation*, p. 428.

find a channel of communication for itself, no matter how stupendous the cost.

When, therefore, we ask what Jesus of Nazareth did for forgiveness, we may assert unhesitatingly that he convinced men of God's readiness to forgive.

(2) He also quickened and intensified humanity's sense of sinfulness.

We do not realize how soiled a garment is until it is compared with one that is stainless. We learn how crooked a stick is when it is placed by the side of one absolutely straight. It is the most brilliant light which casts the deepest shadow. When the Light of the World came, then men saw in most definite outline the shadow resting upon humanity. The contrast between his perfect rectitude and their distorted lives made them painfully aware how unseemly their characters were. His spotless purity startlingly revealed their sin-stains. That the Athenians could not tolerate the best man who ever walked their streets — but compelled Socrates to drink the hemlock — is the most searching insight one can get into the infirmities of the Greek character. That Jesus of Nazareth, humanity at its best, could live only three years of public life in Palestine is the clearest revelation possible of the perversion of the moral sense of his generation; and the conviction that if he had come to any other generation or country his fate would have been substantially the same gives to us our most impressive illustration of the sinfulness of human nature.

That the coming of Jesus Christ into the world has deepened men's consciousness of the exceeding sinfulness of sin there can be no doubt. It is seen in a more sober view of life; in the penitential note of our hymns; in the aspirations embodied in architecture; in the exertions of philanthropists to save men from evil. Sin is made known only by contrast. When all is dark, a shadow is not seen. Jesus in revealing the splendor of righteousness made manifest the nature of sin. His holiness was itself the severest condemnation of sin and a vindication of the divine character.

Jesus upheld the sanctions of the moral world and at the same time condemned sin by his words. When he spoke of God it was as the Holy Father. The first petition of his prayer was, "Hallowed be thy name," indicating that the primary desire of his life was that the divine holiness might be perceived and honored. His words against militant iniquity were as hot, terrible, and unsparing as a bolt of lightning. Sin is so horrible a thing that rather than commit it one is to cut off his hand or pluck out his eye. It is better to die than to give offense. By every word of his mouth Jesus exalted righteousness and denounced unrighteousness.

By his actions he condemned sin. He came into the world to save men from it. All his persuasions were to induce men to leave it. The purpose of his life was to win a victory over it. He obeyed God's holy law, he honored it by following it implicitly, and rather than be disobedient, he went to his death. God's will must be done, however costly the sacrifice required. The entire life of Jesus, as it is recorded in the Gospels, is an ever-increasing revelation of the authority and glory of righteousness and of God's hatred of unrighteousness.

But it is chiefly in the consciousness of the Master that we see the unveiling of iniquity and behold it in its naked ugliness. He who would be the mediator between God and man in the supreme transaction of forgiveness must know what sin is in all its hideousness; he must feel its sickening and utter wretchedness; he must appreciate to the full its relentless malignity. He who would make an atonement for sin must realize the sin in the height of its pride and in the depth of its woe; he must feel its burden upon his own soul. How else can he reveal it adequately to men? In what other way can he make men feel that his work is genuine? Hence it is that we find in the sorrow Jesus felt in the presence of sin the most impressive revelation of the character of evil.

The reader will remember that Milton, in his

delineation of sin, described it at first in its heroic aspects. Satan was an archangel in form and power. He elicits our admiration as he challenges the supremacy of heaven's Eternal King. As he continues in evil he loses his glory, becomes more cunning, reptilian, loathsome, until finally he and all his followers are changed into serpents greedily devouring illusions. Thus does the poet describe the career of sin from its pride to its despicableness, from its glory to its shame.

Jesus encountered sin in all of these aspects. He first met it in a mighty battle for vast issues. In the wilderness he was tempted by the Prince of this world, and the wager was a world-wide and age-long empire. It was a contest with colossal powers for imperial results. As he lived more deeply into the world's evil, sin changed its form; it expressed itself in the craft of the Pharisee, the fickleness of the people, the treachery of friends, and the viperous cunning of the priests. Judas, and not the great hierarch of darkness, is the type of evil. The Christ goes more deeply yet, even to the bottom of the abyss, and knows sin in its most dismal woe, feeling the utter horror and God-forsakenness of it. The agony of Gethsemane was not the penal infliction which an indignant God visited upon him, neither was it a legal condemnation which he bore. It was the Holy One feeling the weight of the world's sin upon his own pure soul. The realization of its pitiless malignity, its sullen ingratitude, its sterile wretchedness, swept over him like a flood. It was more than a consciousness of the sins of the priests, the baseness of Judas, the dullness of his disciples; it was a sense of the world's iniquity, of the depths of humanity's degradation, of the enormity of it all in the sight of God. No wonder that he sweat great drops of blood as in the white light of his own holiness he entered into the vastness and the sickening horror of the world's transgressions. Again upon the cross a black cloud drifted up from the abyss, and as the dripping gloom and biting darkness encompassed him, he tasted sin's utter godlessness.

The writer of the epistle to the Hebrews tells us that Jesus tasted death for every man, and Paul adds that the sting of death is sin. The bitterness of the cup which the Father would not take from the lips of his Son was not the pains of death; it was a consciousness of the sin of the world,— a perception of what sin means to God, and of what it is in its essential nature.

It is by this knowledge that the righteous servant justifies many. By his knowledge of our guilt he becomes our High Priest, our Interpreter. He interprets the holiness of God and the needs of man. Whoever now comes to Christ in faith knows his sin as he never knew it before; he perceives its deformity and guilt, he learns to look upon it as God looks upon it. He hates it and turns from it. He also sees by our Lord's words, by the purpose of his life, and especially by his sufferings in the presence of sin and under its weight, the ineffable holiness of God. Man never would have felt that his sins were forgiven, had he not seen in all the activities and feelings of Jesus an adequate consciousness of the essential nature of human guilt. But this clear consciousness is seen in all Christ's actions from the manger to the cross. In the fine words of Martineau: "The humility of Christ betrays a mind profoundly impressed with a sense of evil and the universality of sin. Beginning with the call to repentance, and expiring with the prayer of forgiveness, he seems never to have quitted the presence of human guilt, and everywhere to have fixed upon it the same full, clear, unconscious look, divinely earnest and divinely sad."

Trusting in God's readiness to forgive, as attested by our Lord's consciousness of divine Fatherhood, knowing the truth about sin by his words, his life, and his sufferings, beholding the holiness of the Father in his character and his obedience, the sinful soul can believe itself forgiven. It knows God's mercy, it knows his holiness, it knows the character of sin.

It is not infrequently affirmed that the revelation of the character of God which Jesus made is the chief power in leading men to repentance.

This assertion is not borne out by our investigation. Both in literature and in life the fell results of wrong-doing first awaken the slumbering soul and turn its steps toward righteousness. When it faces in a new direction, and confronts a fresh light, the sense of personal guilt increases, and repentance is perfected; but penitence is seldom originated by the sight of the greatness of love.

Taking this idea into the realm of faith, we shall find, if I mistake not, that most men who are living sinful lives either do not hear the preaching of the love of God in Jesus Christ, or, if they hear, are but little impressed. While their wills are centred upon other things it is impossible for them to have any compelling realization of either the compassion of God or what sin costs him. Their perception of all the divine realities is dim. The forces which will stir them to repentance are the pains of violated law, the retributions which follow evil courses. The soul thus quickened may behold God's mercy as made known in Jesus, and begin a holy life. Then the knowledge of what sin meant to Jesus will enkindle a sense of guilt and make repentance complete. In the forgiveness of sin it is the work of the Spirit to convict of sin, of righteousness, and of judgment; it is the work of the historical Jesus of Nazareth to make repentance perfect by deepening the sense of personal unworthiness, and to bring home to the penitent the wickedness of sin, and the righteousness and mercy of God.

It is difficult accurately to distinguish, even in thought, between the work of the historical Jesus in forgiveness and that of the Eternal Christ. This we are endeavoring to do, even though imperfectly, in order to make more salient the truths to be touched upon in the next chapter. The fact to which we are about to call attention involves both the work of Jesus and of the Eternal Spirit. Coming within the circle of light which streams from Jesus of Nazareth, in its solemn glory a contrite man sees himself as he is, and beholds the holiness and gentleness of God. Entering into the consciousness of Jesus, he knows himself forgiven. All the conditions of forgiveness are there.

But the soul is an absorbent. It is easily saturated with the personal influence of another. Coming thus near to Jesus in faith, the penitent puts on our Lord's character, he becomes a new creature, he is saved both from the love of sin and the power of sin; he is redeemed by the divine energy. This transforming process gives him another assurance of forgiveness. He perceives that with this new attitude of mind, standing within the play of redemptive force, he will attain to the Master's likeness. He is united to one who will perfect him in all holiness. Thus his faith becomes prophetic of righteousness; it is essential righteousness. His faith, to use Paul's legal phraseology, takes away all judicial condemnation, and puts him in the relationship to God of a son. He becomes one with God in character.

How does the historical Jesus of Nazareth mediate our forgiveness?

(1) He reveals and makes effective God's eagerness to forgive and reconcile us unto himself. Jesus did not make God willing to forgive, but he manifested that forgiveness.

(2) By his words, the sacrifice of his life, and his spiritual consciousness he discloses the essential wickedness of sin and the divine condemnation of it; and thus makes known and exalted the holiness of God.

(3) Whenever any one turns to Jesus in penitence, he is brought into such an attitude of mind toward sin, and has formed within him such a sense of the worth of righteousness, that genuine forgiveness is possible.

Jesus does something for us which we could not do for ourselves. He declares to us how God looks upon sin. He unveils the sanctity of the moral world. He makes it possible for God fully to pardon us. Many writers on the atonement object to the statement that Jesus removed any obstacle to our forgiveness. But surely there are certain conditions to be fulfilled before forgiveness can flow from God to man. For these conditions the work of Jesus provided. He set forth the chief factors which enter into pardon — love, holiness, sin — in their true nature. He wrought a work in our interest, — a work, as it were, outside of us, without which God could not consistently have forgiven us.

(4) Jesus of Nazareth does something *in* us, as well as *for* us. We have a right thus to distinguish in Christian experience, and it helps to clearness of thought. When we come into the circle of his light he impresses himself upon us, we are clothed with his character, we are changed into his likeness. In him we achieve oneness with God.

If it be objected that the cross has not been given its Scriptural prominence in this interpretation of the work of him who hung upon it, the reply is that in the mind of the writer the cross is not something to be considered apart from the life and spiritual consciousness of Jesus. Rather it is the focus of all the truths and forces we have been considering. It was at the cross that the divine love made its consummate revelation. It was at the cross that the divine holiness flashed forth in most awful light. It was at the cross that the degradation and malignity of sin reached its most damning manifestation.

The cross is the symbol of Christianity, and the doctrine of the death of the Christ the heart of the gospel, not because it contains something separable in nature from the other forms of our

Lord's activity, but because these were there symbolized with dramatic intensity. The sacrificial death of Jesus was not the work he accomplished, it was the *via dolorosa* along which he toiled in fulfillment of his task. Love can reveal itself to the utmost only by the complete surrender of life. The cross grew out of the wrath of man and the necessity for infinite love to reveal itself in the most unmistakable way. The spot where the fullness of love meets the supreme virulence of sin must be marked by a cross.

If this interpretation of the work of Jesus seems inadequate to any reader who has followed me thus far, I hope his patience will endure through the next chapter, where perhaps he will find recognized and treated what he has here missed.

IV

WHAT DOES THE ETERNAL CHRIST DO FOR OUR RECONCILIATION?

The Eternal Spirit has his task in the revelation of the mind and heart of God to mankind, and only God, operating through the entire term of history, can achieve God's work. — GEORGE A. GORDON.

For if the blood of goats and bulls, and the ashes of a heifer sprinkling them that have been defiled, sanctify unto the cleanness of the flesh: how much more shall the blood of Christ, who through the eternal Spirit offered himself without blemish unto God, cleanse your conscience from dead works to serve the living God? — EPISTLE TO THE HEBREWS.

CHAPTER IV

WHAT DOES THE ETERNAL CHRIST DO FOR OUR RECONCILIATION?

EVEN though forgiveness is complete, there are limits beyond which it cannot go. It cannot undo the fact of sin. It cannot efface the memory of evil done. It cannot hold in leash the consequences of wrong which are now spreading their destruction. It cannot quench the fires of remorse or stifle regret. Evidently a believer is not saved until he is purged from an evil conscience and his memory is cleansed. The atonement as thus far discussed simply shows how the will is made accordant with the divine purpose, and the heart returns an answering affection for a love that has been freely poured out in its behalf. If the believer were an isolated individual, bound by relationships only to the Almighty Father, a discussion of the atonement need go no further than to show how the prodigal is brought home again and is made a partaker of the Father's bounty. Beyond this partial salvation for the individual few interpretations of the atonement go. After reading many books on all phases of the subject, I do not recall a single modern treatise which carries the discussion beyond the forgiveness and healing of the individual. This would be sufficient, perchance, if the single soul, in being redeemed, were deprived of memory; if salvation blotted out all his recollections of the guilty past; or else so encased him in selfishness that the consequences of his evil deeds in the lives of others were to him a matter of no concern. But in Christian experience just the contrary is true. The nearer one approaches the splendor of the Eternal Light, the blacker do the sins of the past life appear. The more one enters into the mind of Christ, the greater is his concern for those whom he has wronged. He thinks less of personal bliss, and becomes more solicitous for those whom his evil actions have injured. The omission to study the problem of reconciliation in the light of man's relationship to his fellows, as well as in the light of his relationship to God, is all the more inexplicable because one of the pronounced characteristics of modern life is its social consciousness. Never was the feeling of human brotherhood stronger; never did men more thoroughly understand the principle that none liveth to himself and none dieth to himself; never has the assertion been more positive that the individual cannot be saved alone; never has less attention been paid to legal, governmental, expiatory aspects of the atonement; never has so much thought been given to the interpretation of religious truth in the light of man's recognized spiritual needs. Yet no recent writer on the atonement has ever lifted his eyes from the individual transgressor. Apparently these modern theologians find nothing in the one man to be regenerated but the heart and will. They have no word about the memory. One searches in vain for a single reflection on the possibility of dwelling in the glory of the presence of God with the recollection of an unholy past. One might infer from reading the latest books on the subject that when a man repents of his sins and turns from them he is freed from all responsibility for those he has wronged, and that in rapturous bliss and utter forgetfulness he enters into the peace of perfect reconciliation. The older theologians, whom we so often charge with preaching an individualistic gospel, had in their minds a very distinct notion of the sin of the world. It was an entity which must be met and settled with; and to the best of their ability, and according to their light, they showed how Christ's suffering on the cross balanced the world's iniquity. Our newer religious thinking starts with the assumption of the closeness of man's relations to his fellows; it analyzes and proclaims the social consciousness; and yet there probably was never a time in the history of religious thought when the atonement has been discussed in a way so baldly individualistic.

How much greater the problem of reconciliation is than recent writers have recognized is made clear by a simple illustration. The parable of the Prodigal Son is often quoted as an example of the simplicity of the gospel. It is a beautiful setting forth of the truth of God's readiness to pardon, but it does not pretend to embody the whole process of reconciliation. Like most parables, it expounds only a phase of truth. Let us suppose that the prodigal has a younger brother whom he takes with him from his father's home, leading the boy into the dens of vice and teaching him the ways of debauchery. By and by the prodigal comes to himself and says, "I will arise and go to my father," and, as we know, he is received with joy and eager forgiveness. The lad, however, who was so easily enticed into sin is not so readily induced to forsake it. He stubbornly refuses to return with the prodigal, and goes into deeper and more perverse iniquity. Is the prodigal comfortable in his new robe and jeweled ring, amid the merriment of the banquet? Will not the memory of his brother, whom his own willfulness has led astray, shadow his heart and make perfect peace impossible? And the father, while he may have freely forgiven the prodigal, can he be perfectly reconciled to him so long as the lad is out in the darkness? There is no peace for the prodigal until there is an atonement for his memory. His father may forgive him, but he cannot forgive himself. He is not redeemed from his sin while the guilt of it, or the shadow of the guilt, lies on his conscience. The father also, who loves the lad equally with the prodigal, cannot contemplate the latter with perfect complacency in unequivocal reconciliation so long as the consequences of the prodigal's insubordination are visited upon the younger boy. The supreme purpose of his life as a father has been thwarted. He may school himself to submit to a fate which has broken and disappointed his life, but if he sees no further than the wrecking of his hopes, he has no profound blessedness. Both will leave their home and search for the wanderer, and do all for him that compassionate love can suggest and human power carry out. Either the lad will be brought again to his home, saved through his hard experience, inflexibly dedicated to virtue because his eyes have been opened to the nature of sin, and made more appreciative of his father's love by his sojourn in the wilderness; or, in some way which we cannot well imagine, it will be made apparent to both father and son that out of the evil greater good has come, and that the wrath of man has wrought eternal praise to God. In the light of this vision, or in the joy of the actual redemption of the lost one, perfect reconciliation is possible. Then the fires of remorse are quenched, the memory is cleansed of its dead weight, the conscience is at peace with itself, and the supreme purpose of life is seen to be fulfilled, not blighted.[1]

We venture another pertinent illustration to enforce this truth. We may imagine that after Jacob's sons had sold their brother into Egypt, they repented and confessed their fault, and the old patriarch forgives them; but forgiveness, even though genuine, would have come far short of reconciliation. Complacency of mind, the joy of unshadowed union with his sons, is impossible while the thought remains of his younger son toiling in slavery and perhaps hopelessly crippled in his mental and moral nature. The reconciliation of Jacob to his sons is dependent on whether or not Joseph is hopelessly lost. When, however, he sees that evil has been made in God's wise providence to work good, then an abundant and unreserved accord is possible with those who have wronged him. Judah and his brethren, by the same knowledge, are enabled to be reconciled to their past.

The horror of sin is its contagious nature. The pestilence passes from the diseased one into the community. It is unconfined. A wrong committed sends its waves of destruction rolling on in ever widening circles and with accumulated power

---

[1] The responsibility of the younger brother for his own sin does not entirely free the prodigal, and it is his reconciliation we are considering.

to the ends of the earth, overwhelming guilty and innocent, and working havoc down through the generations. A gospel of the atonement is singularly parochial which covers only the relations of the individual with God. If the blight of sin never passed beyond the evil-doer, then the killing of the love and power of it in the individual by genuine contrition, and a return to a God solicitous to forgive, would be the easy solution of the whole matter. But the dreadful characteristic of sin is that its effects are visited upon others. No man liveth, or sinneth, to himself. He drags others with him into the pit. The believer cannot escape from his deeds as the butterfly from its cocoon. There are accounts to be settled and amends to be made. A gospel which tells the perpetrator how to escape from the murky stream of iniquity where his victims are still struggling, and promises to make him stand in Zion and before God in rapturous joy, with no smoking mount of horror in his memory, is anæmic in the extreme. "Son, remember," were the solemn words which Abraham spoke to Dives in torment. It is because we must remember that we need an atonement which deals not only with the love and power of sin in our wills and hearts, but with the evil which has gone out from our infirmity and perversity into the world. The difficulty of conquering sin in the individual is great, but greater is the need of checking the results of sin as it moves on in its destructive course. Most explanations of the atonement go no further than to make plain the method by which the root of sin is destroyed in the individual heart. But this is the smaller part of the problem. When one repents of sin, he does not lightly shake off his responsibility for its effects upon others. He cannot in the eyes of men,—certainly he cannot in the sight of God. It is he who has done this evil. It is he who launched it into the world, and it is he who must bear the guilt of it. In the foregoing chapter we insisted strongly that there could be no genuine repentance or pardon without adequate knowledge of the sanctity of moral obligation and the hideousness of sin. In this chapter we would contend just as emphatically that there can be no *reconciliation* without either a *knowledge* of how the dreadful effects of sin are caught up in some providential way and made to subserve a good purpose, or an unquestioning *faith* that in the goodness of God this will be done.

The Buddhists have a doctrine of Karma. It means the sum total of a man's life, his thoughts, deeds, influence. It is the result of a person's existence taken as a whole. It includes what he is and what he has done. It is the net product of his being and activity.

Every treatment of the atonement which considers man apart from Karma, which declares him saved while paying no attention to the aggregate of his life, is painfully lame and unsatisfactory. To any earnest man who thinks of something more than the salvation of his own soul, and wishes to undo his mistakes and make good any wrong he may have committed, the foremost desire is to be assured that God in Christ provides for the evil that has gone out from him. He wants to know that there is a salvation comprehensive enough to embrace both himself and all the effects of his life. The more unselfish he becomes, the more concerned will he be about the divine provisions for the injury he has wrought in the world. He will care more for this than for his personal blessedness. Not merely the eradication of personal sin, but the cure of cosmical evil is included in a gospel of reconciliation, and a reasoned and sufficient faith in the latter is as indispensable as the experience of the other to the final peace of a redeemed soul. A sinner needs more than forgiveness. He is not saved until some vision or experience of God's grace reconciles him to the total results of his life.

The spiritual need of every believer either to see distinctly the dire effects of his mistakes and transgressions overcome by the good that is in the world, or by faith to enter into the ultimate triumph of the "deep things of God" over the "deep things of Satan," is abundantly certified by the authors we have investigated. Dante entered into the peace of perfect reconciliation when in the Fountain of Living Light he saw what is imperfect here made perfect there, all things being bound with love in one volume. Milton shows that Adam after his transgression was not chiefly solicitous about his personal salvation. The horror of his deed was the woe entailed upon the unborn generations. He was not so slight a creature as to be absorbed in the thought of seeking salvation for his own soul. The commanding article in his reconciliation will be the knowledge of how through his sin grace has much more abounded. His abject despair is changed to rapturous joy as Michael unfolds to his astonished mind the glories of God's redemption through Christ. The final triumph of the Infinite Goodness, which he appropriates by faith, is the ground of his reconciliation with his past. The sons of Jacob, if they ever truly repented of the crime of selling Joseph into slavery, were outside the gates of joy, and under the shadow of a tormenting memory, until they knew that God, working through their crime, had accomplished good.

Sometimes the same problem presents a different aspect. We need a reconcilement with life as we experience it. The innocent, suffering from the follies and perversity of the wicked, cry out for an explanation of the providential order of the world. This is the agony of Job. Stripped of his possessions and all that made life endurable, he is tempted to curse life as he sees it. His peace comes when he can say, "Now mine eye seeth thee." The writer of the Seventeenth Psalm will be satisfied when he beholds God's likeness. Milton acquiesces in his blindness because by waiting in the darkness he understands that he is serving. Whittier can look with serene mind on a world tormented by evil because by spiritual prescience he sees —

> "The patience of immortal love
> Outwearing mortal sin."

He rebels not at the evil which comes to his lot, for he is

> "Assured alone that life and death
> His mercy underlies."

"After all," says Phillips Brooks, "for every trouble and doubt in life, except those which come directly from our own sinfulness, the only consolation which we really need is explanation." There are occasions when we can perceive a definite explanation for a given infliction; then we acquiesce. More often the trial is so woven into the fabric of the providential order that a specific elucidation is impossible; then, like Job, we receive, instead of an explanation, a conviction of the righteousness and goodness of God, and this suffices for our peace. When the evils "come directly from our own sinfulness," we need the same consolation. Either we know that the wrong committed works good, as in the case of Joseph; or by faith we rest in the assurance that God will make the wrath of man to praise him.

One of the deepest spiritual needs of men living in a sinful world is to be reconciled to the results following from their own lives, and cheerfully to acquiesce in the discipline which comes to them so often in the guise of the "slings and arrows of outrageous fortune." To most of us, to accept the hard training of life with serene minds presents a greater difficulty than the problem of the method by which God forgives us. Any explanation of how at-one-ment with God is achieved that leaves out of account cosmical evil and all that it means to us is woefully provincial.

Forgiveness cannot any longer be treated as a judicial acquitment. In so far as we know anything about divine pardon, it is an inner witness of the spirit, giving peace and joy. Every modern doctrine of justification must start, not from the conception of a divine judgment seat and a legal acquittal, but from the interior needs and satisfactions of the human soul. Reconciliation is not a written decree, handed down from the throne room, declaring us free from all debts or penalties. It is a prevailing mood of restfulness, trust, and hope in life as it is and is to be. It is glad acceptance of our experiences and the ways of God. Such reconciliation can only come with the conviction that we are living in a divine universe, and that evil has been or will be overcome by the good.

The authors we have consulted hint at another aspect of evil which must be dealt with in any comprehensive treatment of reconciliation. They explain how the injured one is made complacent with the injurer. Shakespeare indicates that Prospero could be heartily reconciled to those who had wronged him because the soul of goodness had been distilled out of things evil. The Enchanter had so overruled the malignity of his foes that his life had not become the ruin they had plotted, but had accomplished its highest ends. Had his plans and hopes been devastated, and his daughter's career blighted, he could scarcely have been reconciled with the perpetrators of the evil. In the "Paradise Lost" God forgives Adam because he knows his own divine purposes are not thwarted. Were he impotent in the midst of a ruined world, defeated in his cherished designs, while sin rioted in wild triumph, then perfect forgiveness and complete reconciliation would have been a very different matter.

How far have we gone in a doctrine of reconciliation, if we only show how God receives and forgives individual sinners? Can he gather the redeemed about him and look complacently down on a wrecked world, thankful that he has saved so many out of the overwhelming flood of evil? Can God be reconciled with man and the work of man, if his holy purposes are shattered and the sacrifice of his love issues only in irretrievable defeat? It is an axiom in life and in religious thought that there is no reconciliation without satisfaction. The wrong for which there is no spiritual comfort or compensation is a perpetual bar to the union of spiritual beings. The condition upon which God offers blessedness is that his holy will be done, his love be satisfied, his kingdom be established, and that the wrath of man praise him. The Church always assumes this victory of God in all its thinking upon the atonement; and what we involuntarily assume is of fundamental importance. It is the ground upon which the whole superstructure rests. We can build castles in the air if it is not important to regard foundations. If God's love is the basis of forgiveness, so is his dealing with cosmic evil the indispensable factor in reconciliation. To treat of divine pardon without mentioning divine grace is no more inefficient than to discuss the atonement and omit all reference to the necessity both to God and man of the ultimate divine victory over evil.

I think what has been said makes evident that man and God are not reconciled when forgiveness has been given and received. The consequences of sin must be dealt with, the memory cleansed, the mind made acquiescent with the providential order of the world. Reconciliation cannot be considered apart from the problem of cosmic evil. Man cannot be reconciled with his past without a faith that God makes the wrath of man to praise him. He cannot be reconciled to the woes of life unless he is convinced that all things work together for good. Neither, reasoning from human analogy, can God be reconciled to man, if his plans are frustrated by the evil of the world. His reconciliation, like man's, depends on how evil is dealt with.

What principle or unquestioned teaching is there in the Christian faith which has to do with the problem of cosmic evil? If we can find it, its contemplation will be a Lethe to heal the tortured memory of believers. Its reality is the basis upon which God is reconciled to man. The answer is not far to seek. A cosmic Christ is Christianity's solution of cosmic evil.

The men who followed Jesus of Nazareth were content at first to consider him as an extraordinary prophet. But as the full significance of the grace and beauty that was in him began to unfold itself to their minds, they could not think of him as being explained by any temporal designation. The strange light that was in him was not human brilliancy; it represented and revealed an eternal reality. His glory was not of the earth, earthy; it was from heaven; it was the glory of the only begotten of the Father, the express image of the Godhead. What he was

God had always been. To Paul Christ was a spiritual principle; "in him were all things created in the heavens and upon the earth, things visible and things invisible, whether thrones, or dominions, or principalities, or powers. All things have been created through him and unto him, and he is before all things and in him all things consist."[1] Again, in the earlier letter to the Corinthians, speaking of the experiences of the Israelites in the wilderness and their spiritual sustenance, he had said: "For they drank of a spiritual rock that followed them; and the rock was Christ."[2] The prologue of the Gospel of John sweeps up into the same lofty region of thought: "In the beginning was the Word, and the Word was with God, and the Word was God. . . . All things were made by him, and without him was not anything made that hath been made. . . . He was in the world, and the world was made by him, and the world knew him not. . . . And the Word became flesh and dwelt among us, and we beheld his glory, the glory of the only begotten of the Father, full of grace and truth."[3] In the book of the Revelation Christ is referred to as "the Lamb that hath been slain from the foundation of the world."[4] The Greek fathers, yielding to that inevitable tendency of mind to recognize in Jesus the image of the Eternal,

---

[1] Col. i, 16–17. [2] 1 Cor. x, 4.
[3] John i, 1 ff. [4] Rev. xiii, 8.

declared that the passion of Christ was a sacrament, a mystery of eternal truth, a visible sign of a great supra-temporal act. Christian thinkers early elaborated the thought that in God there is the perpetually human. There is in him that which is akin to humanity; a nature that created us, that is in close touch with our needs, in which we subsist, and by which we are redeemed.

For clearness of thought many Christian thinkers have differentiated God as revealed to humanity from the Infinite Abyss of Being who is unsearchable. This God who is beyond the compass of our thought or experience we call the Father. God, as he discloses himself in humanity, we designate as "the Word," "the Son," or, when we refer to his highest self-disclosure, we say "the Christ." When we think of God not as the Source of all things, nor as a Redeemer, but as the Spirit operating within us, then we denominate him the Holy Spirit. Our theologians are not always clear, either in their thought or their definitions, of these different aspects of God's self-declaration, but there is no mistaking Christianity's constant assertion that God is in the world, reconciling it unto himself.

As this eternal forth-putting of God, "the Word," "the Son," came to its richest and consummate expression in Jesus, the Christ, believers express this identity of the historical and the Everlasting by the use of the designation, "the

Eternal Christ." The Eternal Christ is the spirit of Jesus in its infinite nature. By this ever-present Christ were all things created. More important is the statement that "in him all things consist." Every human being depends on him, as every wave depends upon the ocean. Like the trees nourished in the soil, we are rooted in him. He is in all, and over all, and working through all. He is the life of every holy aspiration, the pain in every twinge of remorse, the calm of a quiet mind. Being then, so to speak, that part of God which is ever present in the processes of nature and history, that fringe of the Eternal Abyss which comes in contact with the shore, that elemental life out of which humanity came and which sustains each individual spirit, — being thus inextricably associated with mankind, he must suffer. The sufferings of God in the eternal forth-putting of himself which we call Christ is a distinctive doctrine of Christianity.

Our modern faith does not shrink from proclaiming a thorough-going doctrine of the incarnation. The Eternal Son does not look upon the woes of men sympathetically, as a traveler might sorrow over the destitution of a Turkish village. He identifies himself with our life because one with us, enters into the state of retributive disorder, abides here, and suffers until he overcomes evil. He did not meet the corporate woe at one point, and then escape from the load. His iden-

THE ETERNAL CHRIST AND RECONCILIATION 231

tification with humanity is perpetual. Being always in man and for man, he is hurt by every sin of man, he feels the sting of every evil, the chastisement of every wrong is upon him.

This thought of God as so identified with man that in all our afflictions he is afflicted was a staggering one to the ancient mind, trained in the philosophy of Greece. Tennyson has finely rendered the common feeling about the gods:[1]

> "who haunt
> The lucid interspace of world and world,
> Where never creeps a cloud, or moves a wind,
> Nor ever falls the least white star of snow,
> Nor ever lowest roll of thunder moans,
> Nor sound of human sorrow mounts to mar
> Their sacred, everlasting calm."

But once conceive a compassion in God tender as that of Jesus, and consider sin to be as black as it appeared on Calvary, and such love must be thought of as forever suffering for the evils of the world. Infinite love is not above the stars, but close against sin, tasting its bitterness, enduring its drenching misery, subduing its malignity. And when sin and love meet in such intimate and genuine conflict, there must be a burden of woe borne by sympathetic and militant love. Such pity as Jesus felt for the wretchedness of mankind was not a fleeting disposition of an exceptional heart; it is as eternal as the nature of God. The forgiving mercy of Jesus was more than an ema-

[1] Lucretius.

nation from the nobility of his soul, it was an expression of what is everlasting in the Father; the radiant holiness in him was a flash from the never-setting Sun of Righteousness. Conceive of the nature of Jesus as eternal in its essence, and a belief in the passibility of God is unavoidable. Christ, the self-expression of God in time, must have suffered from the foundation of the world, and he will suffer so long as men sin. Every human affliction is felt by Christ. We endure in our person and fortunes the recoil of our own transgressions; but Christ is really taking upon himself the sins of the world. He is being wounded to-day for our transgressions; he is being bruised by every one of our iniquities. The chastisement of our peace is upon him, and by his stripes we are healed. In Jesus of Nazareth the Eternal Word felt the pangs of the cross. But that three hours' pain was not a spasm ending in unbroken joy. It was symbolical of a perpetual feeling. What Jesus experienced in spiritual revulsion from sin, and his suffering on its behalf, is a revelation of an unchanging consciousness in God. As the flash of the volcano discloses for a few hours the elemental fires at the earth's centre, so the light on Calvary was the bursting forth through historical conditions of the very nature of the Everlasting. There was a cross in the heart of God before there was one planted on the green hill outside of Jerusalem. And now that the cross of wood has been taken down, the one in the heart of God abides, and it will remain so long as there is one sinful soul for whom to suffer.

This would be a dreadful doctrine if the pain were helpless agony, if it were only impotent sorrow whose lengthened woe issued in defeat. The Christian doctrine of God would be inferior to that of the Greeks, did it not supplement this teaching of the infinite passibility of God with the assertion that the Almighty abides in perfect felicity. In him is completeness of joy because he sees the end from the beginning. He knows the final result, and in this perfect knowledge there is fullness of peace. The sorrow is submerged in joy. The sea of glass is mingled with fire.

The immanent Christ, who lives and suffers in every child of man, and who came to highest expression in Jesus of Nazareth, is enduring a constant passion. Part we know in our own experience, and are thus made partakers of his sufferings. Part is deeper than any human consciousness; it is the unshared sorrow of the Eternal Redeemer, but it is not fruitless agony. It is the pain of a process which ends in a glorious consummation. The meaning of the twilight darkness is fulfilled in the joy of the morning. Jesus of Nazareth never placed the significance of the crucifixion in its agonies. As he stood before the cross in that last fateful week in Jerusalem, in three flashing sentences he disclosed the relation of Calvary to the sins of the world: "Now is condemnation come into the world;" that is, the cross makes known and condemns sin. "Now is the prince of this world cast out;" in the cross sin is conquered. "And I, if I be lifted up from the earth, will draw all men unto myself;"[1] the revelation of the cross is the persuasive power which brings all men to God. The apostolic church spoke often of the Master's passion, but it was to show why it behooved Christ to suffer. For the joy that was set before him he endured the cross, despising shame.[2] He was incarnated "that through death he might bring to naught him that had the power of death, that is, the devil."[3] The work of Jesus upon earth is the perpetual task of the living Christ. He is through all the struggling and grief-shadowed ages enduring the cross, not in hopeless pain, but for the joy of a completed work. Through this constant death he is bringing to naught the forces and relicts of evil.

The triumph of Jesus is predicted with perfect confidence in the New Testament. It is needless to multiply passages. The following will readily occur to the reader. In Revelation the Lamb that had been slain is seated in the midst of the throne, and on his head are many crowns. He nailed the old ordinances to the cross, "having

[1] John xii, 31-32.   [2] Heb. xii, 2.   [3] Heb. ii, 14.

put off from himself the principalities and powers, he made a show of them openly, triumphing over them in it."[1] Paul declares that the crucified Christ is risen, and that he must reign until all things have been subjected unto him, "that God may be all in all."[2] This is fulfilled in the work of the immanent and transcendent Christ, "who created all things, and in whom all things consist." "For it was the good pleasure of the Father that in him should all fulness dwell; and through him to reconcile all things unto himself, having made peace through the blood of his cross; through him, I say, whether things upon earth or things in the heavens."[3] It is God's good pleasure "to sum up all things in Christ, the things in heaven and the things upon earth."[4]

We are not to suppose the great apostle is teaching here anything so crude and artificial as that the literal blood of Jesus of Nazareth made peace between God and man. The blood symbolizes the sacrificial life. But to Paul the life of Christ was not confined to thirty-three years of an earthly ministry. It began before time was; in him all things consist; his ever-suffering and finally victorious power is toiling through the ages, overcoming all evil, wiping out the vestiges of sin, subduing all things unto himself until he works an actual reconciliation of all things in

---

[1] Col. ii, 14–15.   [2] 1 Cor. xv, 25 ff.
[3] Col. i, 19–20.   [4] Eph. i, 10.

himself, and all conscious beings recognize their life in him. In him they come to their perfection and enter into peace.

All things actually subsist in this immanent, eternal Christ. The redeemed are they who by faith perceive and acquiesce in this relationship, and so find their lives hid with Christ in God, rooted and grounded in the soil of his sacrificial nature. In him they have their most poignant sense of personal unworthiness; in him they see God's righteous forgiveness; in him, like Dante in his beatific vision, they behold life with all its mistakes, sins, devastations to be encompassed and transfigured by the conquering love of God. To them everywhere in this universe the light of the glory of God is seen to shine, for God is known to be all and in all.

What the ultimate victory of the immanent Christ implies we are not rash enough to assert. We may hope it means universal salvation and the restoration of all wandering souls; or belief in conditional immortality may give to Christ's triumph another significance. The contents of this idea are beyond our ken. All that is here affirmed is that both the Scriptures and the Christian faith teach that the living Christ will completely subdue all evil, and that sin will be so dealt with and its consequences so expunged that every living creature will be satisfied. God's holy love will indeed appear to be in all things.

THE ETERNAL CHRIST AND RECONCILIATION 237

This victory over sin and its consequences — this satisfactory dealing with cosmical evil by the suffering strength of the eternal Christ — is an essential part of the atonement. Without it there may be forgiveness, but there is no reconciliation. God's holy love is the cause, Christ's supra-temporal sufferings are essential to the process, but the ultimate victory is not a negligible factor. May we not justly describe it as the ground of reconciliation?

God must be satisfied! This assertion has rung through every great theory of the atonement. How he is satisfied has been explained according to the prevailing ideas of the age. In the time of chivalry his personal honor was shown to be appeased, by either the plenary or adequate suffering of Christ; in the days of juster government the majesty of the law was declared to be vindicated; interpreted in its priestly aspect, Christ's work was a full repentance and confession of humanity's sinfulness. To the modern Christian, trained to think of God as a Father, satisfaction comes through the expression and activity of his compassion. The interpretation here made carries this thought to its full meaning. What satisfies God is the glorious accomplishment of his work in creation and redemption. His plans are fulfilled, his love achieves its perfect work; in no part of the universe is his glory dimmed. Nothing less than this would satisfy God. Forgiveness might be possible, but not reconciliation, if he must sit desolate on his throne amid his ruined worlds while evil holds high carnival. If sin fatally obstructs his benevolent designs, thwarts his purposes, hopelessly blots his fair creation, surely God is not satisfied; neither can he be reconciled to the authors of this perpetual outrage. If we have a right to interpret in any way divine things by human, — and this is our only method of understanding the spiritual world,— then God can be neither satisfied nor reconciled unless his benevolent purposes in creation are consummated.

Neither can a man be fully redeemed unless the Eternal Christ is victor. His will may be atoned and his heart have perfect love, but peace is impossible if the memory holds the past unrelieved. The mind must be purged of an evil conscience; the "stuff'd bosom" cleansed of the "stuff that weighs upon the heart." There must be a Lethe in whose clear waves the black color of the past will fade. There is but one River of Forgetfulness that is sufficient. When, like Dante, we bathe our eyes in the River of Light and see the triumph of the kingdom, we shall be at peace. If we knew that our sins were to go on forever unchecked, that others were perpetually to suffer through our faithlessness, that the footprints of our sin were never to be effaced, and that the consequences were to roll on in ever destructive power, then there would remain no rest for the people of God. The prodigal could not feast in the Father's house for the memory of those he had led into sin.

What will satisfy man, and purge his memory without destroying it? There is but one answer. In this world by faith he will lay hold of the triumph of Christ. He will believe that all things work together for good, and that God makes the wrath of man to praise him. He will rest trustfully on the promise that God in Christ has taken up even his sin and all its consequences into an unchangeable redemptive purpose, and that the will of God will be done. In this faith he has peace. What he cannot do for himself the ever-living and ever-victorious Christ will do for him. He reposes on the divine grace, not merely because it is grace, but because it is divine and therefore triumphant. He beholds Christ actually bearing his transgressions, taking literally the terrible consequences upon himself, and so carrying them as to annul them. This is the believer's peace; it is the reconciliation with his past into which he enters by faith.

It is also his reconciliation with all the disasters and evil of his life. This faith in the triumph of God has always been the hope and joy of the Christian. Without it there is no reconciliation, no peace. In the world to come, faith is changed to vision. In the splendor of the perfect light our sins and their entailment of evil would seem woeful beyond description, were it not that we shall behold them in the sea of Christ's overwhelming and victorious love. Where sin has abounded grace will be seen to have much more abounded, and the glory of grace will cause even the blackness of sin to shine.

Assuredly, the victory of Christ over evil is as essential a part of the atonement as his sufferings. The triumph of the cross is no more to be left out of sight in a discussion of the atonement than are its sorrows. The end is as important as the means. The result of the battle has as much to do with the success of the cause as the methods by which it is fought. The Christ indwelling in humanity accepts the consequences of our sin into his own heart and life, and makes them his. He assumes them, bears them for us, feels their weight. But coming against his strength, their power is stayed, they are buried in the sea of his might, they are trampled under his feet, they are perfectly subdued. This is not rhetoric, but observed fact. There is a *vis medicatrix* in society. A power not ourselves is working for righteousness. The sins of the fathers are visited upon the children unto the third and fourth generation, but the good is transmitted for thousands of generations, for it is supplemented and preserved by the nature of things, which is good. Everywhere we find ourselves in the presence of an immense healing power. When the body is wounded, the remedial forces of nature begin their cleansing and restorative processes. When the soul receives a fearful hurt, the treasuries of peace and strength are hard by. What seemed at the moment to be irretrievable disaster is found to contain the elements of great good. For a true soul every fall may become a fall upward, every loss may be made to produce a high result in gain. Working through all things there is a Reason, an ever unfolding Righteousness, a purifying and sustaining Goodness.

This indwelling God, whom because most fully manifested to us by Jesus of Nazareth, we call the living Christ, is making an actual atonement. He is not doing something legal and forensic which the Father accepts as the best that can be done, and on the ground of which he is reconciled. The immanent, suffering, and victorious Christ is doing a genuine work; he is healing the disease of sin, he is emending its destructive effects. He is cleansing what has been stained, and making whole what has been severed. And his work will continue until this fair universe is what the Creator intended it to be. The fullness of God shall be in all things, the glory of God shall everywhere shine undimmed, and the will of God shall everywhere be done. Faith in this is the peace and reconciliation of the saints. Its accomplishment is the satisfaction of God. It is his reconciliation with whatever the hurt of evil has meant to him. If human sin and its consequences mean anything to the Creator, — and Christian faith instructed at Calvary believes that it means much, — then the divine satisfaction can consist in nothing less than having the suffering for sin culminate in the glorious fulfillment of the purposes of love and righteousness.

The old conception that Jesus in the act and article of his death paid for us a debt which we could not pay for ourselves made a strong appeal for Christian activity. Stronger, however, is the motive which the conception of the progressive, age-long work of a suffering Redeemer calls into life. Faith in Christ, present in the world, bearing our sins, and wounded in all our transgressions, cannot but persuade us, as it did Paul, that it is a privilege to fill up that which is lacking in the afflictions of Christ.[1] We may endure with him the weight of the world's woe; we may be laborers together with him; we may share with him the work of redeeming the world. Our connection with him is real, not sentimental. We are genuine actors on the stage, and upon us rests a heavy responsibility. By our willfulness we

[1] Col. i, 24.

quench his spirit, obstruct his work, lead him anew to Gethsemane. By our faithfulness we glorify him. We augment his efficiency in the world, and hasten the day of his victory. The battle we are fighting is a real one. We are not mimic soldiers, marching and countermarching on a stage. Great issues are being decided by our conduct. If the world battle is won, it will be won in and through humanity. It will be by the divine energy expressing itself through obedient human wills. Man is an indispensable agent in the vast work of healing the open wound of the world. This complete identification of ourselves with Christ in redemption makes a deeper call on our love and energy than does gratitude for a finished work. To us, as to Simon, is given the privilege of helping the Christ bear his cross up Calvary. We carry an actual load, we do right yeoman service, we are partakers of his sufferings, and, therefore, we are with him to behold his glory and have part in the joy of his triumph. To help forward his victory of righteousness has been the aim of the good in all ages. "Socii Dei sumus," said Seneca. Christianity has taken this common instinct, and shown how rich and genuine it is.

In the constant recurrence of the thought that there is a soul of goodness in things evil, the writer would not be understood as taking the position, so forcibly expressed by Emerson, that evil is "good in the making;" nor would he range himself with the Neoplatonists in the optimistic opinion that evil is the necessary foil of good, a mere negative thing, "the shadow of the light." Much so-called evil may doubtless thus be explained; but is it not the more comprehensive and rational view that sin, with its blasting trail of moral evil, is not essential to the universe? Is not sin an irrational and alien thing which is to be got rid of at great cost? There never was an evil action performed but a good one in its place would have led to better results. Sin is wrong, but God's action in reference to it is right, and from right action springs good. The soul of goodness which is in things evil is the presence of the indwelling God, and it is from that fountain of light that the good flows forth, and not from the darkness of the sin. The uplifting power is in the grace that abounds, and is not a constituent part of moral wreckage.

The task to which we set ourselves has now been accomplished. The approach to God's work of reconciliation through Christ by the way of literature and the conscious needs of the human soul rather than along the beaten paths of Scriptural interpretation has been an untried one. Like all new trails blazed through a tangled forest, the path we have cut has doubtless been rough and often obscure. But the work has been worth doing, and if any student of the atonement travels this way again he will have abundant opportunity to make the crooked straight and the obscure plain. The writer's greatest fear is that in his persistent endeavor to be clear he has made his subject matter appear cut and dried. To separate any living thing into its component parts is a deadening process. The soul weaves its mystical fibres into the life of God in so many ways that any attempt to state in the form of principles and systems what is a vital experience appears mechanical and unreal. This limitation, however, rests upon every one who would interpret life in terms of thought. That there may be no misunderstanding of what has been attempted, let us briefly recapitulate the conclusions reached.

We began with the assumption that as Sin, Retribution, and Reconciliation are the themes considered both in the Scriptures and in the supreme works of literature, the poets as well as the apostles might help us to understand what God in Christ did for our reconciliation. We have found that literature sustained the contention of theology that forgiveness, taking place in a moral universe, must be so in accord with righteousness that the sanctity of the moral law shall receive no diminution. With the forgiveness of the individual, and the destruction of the love of sin and its power in him, most theologians stop. Literature and the spiritual needs of one convicted of sin go further. The terrible feature of transgression is its entailment of woe upon others. The consequences of sin must be taken up in any complete solution of the problem of reconciliation. Else man cannot be reconciled to his past; else there is no atonement for his memory; no "enthusiastic temper of espousal" toward life and its disciplinary troubles. Even God cannot be reconciled, if sin eternally thwarts his holy purposes. In a thorough gospel of reconciliation there must not only be forgiveness, but the absolute repose of the mind, both of God and of man, in the divine disposal of sin and its consequences.

In the historical Jesus the free pardon of sin is mediated. This belief is the permanent possession of the church. But Jesus did more. He established the abiding conviction that there are no dates in God's disposition towards men; that there is no time element in his feelings. He disclosed the Father's eternal attitude toward us. He so interpreted and brought near to our sense of need the indwelling God that Christian thinkers have found religious satisfaction in speaking of the immanent God as the Eternal Christ. This designation fits our spiritual necessities. It brings close the humanity of God. It makes him personal, human, understandable. In the living, ever present Christ all things subsist. By repentance and faith we become spiritually one with him. Because we are thus identified with him and share his life we are "accepted in the beloved." We grow up into his likeness, and the atonement becomes an achievement, an at-one-ment with God in Christ.

A further truth urged in this book is that by the Eternal Christ's reconciling work there is an achievement in the world as well as in the individual. As a man's life is inextricably woven into the history of the world, he is not saved apart from others. By faith the individual must enter into Christ's work for the race ere his own soul can be healed. A comprehensive theory of the atonement must consider both the destruction of sin in the heart of the transgressor and the amendment of its consequences in the world. Reconciliation is thus more than forgiveness. It presupposes a harmony which mere pardon cannot accomplish. A repose of man in God like the peace of Jesus in the Father is impossible if on either side there is a tormenting memory of an irremediable wrong. There must be a reconciliation embracing the entire sphere of man's relationship with God. Such a thorough and æonian work must originate with God and be carried on by him. God in Christ is accomplishing in history this reconciliation. His spirit is in humanity. Each wrong thought or deed is a sin against him. He is wounded for our transgressions and bruised for our iniquities. The chastisement of our peace is upon him and by his stripes we are healed. He is bearing our sins and their consequences, not spectacularly, not legally, not forensically, but actually. Yet he is bearing them to some purpose. Immortal love is outwearing mortal sin. This wounded conqueror from Edom is traveling in the greatness of his strength.

Religious thought in the past, in its consideration of reconciliation between God and man, has turned its attention almost exclusively on the significance of the sufferings of Jesus of Nazareth. The older theology affirmed that the agony upon the cross was equivalent to the misery entailed by sin, and therefore satisfied divine justice. Later it was held that God accepted the sacrifice as equivalent to the penalties merited by evil. Then it was maintained that Calvary revealed the nature of evil and the holy love of God. The church has lingered around the cross, absorbed in the contemplation of the sorrows of the Lamb of God, and intent upon explaining their meaning. The contention here made is that, in addition to the revelation of God's grace and man's need, the cross has another significance. To Jesus and to the apostolic church it was the throne of victory; a revelation of spiritual triumph over sin and death. The primitive Christians for four or five centuries never represented the suffering Christ in their catacombs or on their sarcophagi. He was to them the ever-living, glorified, victorious Christ.

We must restore the ancient faith, and magnify the enthroned and sceptred Redeemer. If the cross declares the passion of the eternal love of God, it equally asserts a passion issuing in victory. It leads our thoughts to an eternal, indwelling Christ who is not only bearing our sins, but bearing them away. He is not merely taking the consequences upon himself, he is overcoming the evil of them, making men's mistakes, errors, sins, either to be restrained, or to work out God's redemptive purpose. He is saving the individual, he is also saving the world. He is not suffering expiatory pains which God accepts as an atonement; he is working a real expiation, he is atoning for evil by a counterbalancing good. Upon this conquest of good over evil, reasoning from human analogy, does perfect reconciliation depend. Forgiveness is the outgrowth of penitence accepting holy love, but reconciliation, in the full significance of the word, is conditioned upon the triumph of holy love over the aggregate issue of sin. God is satisfied with nothing less than the complete expression of his love and righteousness carried through to its final purpose. Surely the fulfillment enters into his reconciliation as well as the suffering on the way thither.

This triumph of God's purpose and the accomplishment of his will is the peace of the redeemed. By faith even now we enter into the joy of that victory. We take by faith, while living, our "freehold of thanksgiving." The burden of sin rolls from off our mortal shoulders upon omnipotent strength. One is bearing them who will dispose of them in righteousness. To his resistless grace we trust our past and all its mistakes. Reposing in this supreme Goodness we joyfully accept the stern discipline of the present. In this sure victory of divine love and holiness we rest in perfect trust. Hereafter, when faith has changed to unobstructed vision and we see God face to face, we shall be satisfied with all his ways; with the vision will come a perfect reconciliation.

Some day the church that has lingered weeping at the cross will catch a glimpse of a splendor which will dim the shadow, and with exultant joy will preach the glad tidings that the blood of Christ, offered through the eternal Spirit, is efficacious through all the ages, changing the wrath of man to praise, restraining the residue of evil, and achieving for God and man the great Reconciliation.

Reprint Publishing

For People Who Go For Originals.

This book is a facsimile reprint of the original edition. The term refers to the facsimile with an original in size and design exactly matching simulation as photographic or scanned reproduction.

Facsimile editions offer us the chance to join in the library of historical, cultural and scientific history of mankind, and to rediscover.

The books of the facsimile edition may have marks, notations and other marginalia and pages with errors contained in the original volume. These traces of the past refers to the historical journey that has covered the book.

ISBN 978-3-95940-131-9

Facsimile reprint of the original edition
Copyright © 2015 Reprint Publishing
All rights reserved.

www.reprintpublishing.com

www.ingramcontent.com/pod-product-compliance
Lightning Source LLC
LaVergne TN
LVHW051225080426
835513LV00016B/1420